THE OLD
LAMB & FLAG

The Songs and Story of Preston and its Guild

by

Tom Walsh & Gregg Butler

Carnegie Publishing Ltd., 1992

To the town and people of Preston
for providing between them such an enjoyable place to live.

The Old Lamb and Flag: The Songs and Story of Preston and its Guild

by Tom Walsh and Gregg Butler

Copyright,© Tom Walsh and Gregg Butler, 1992

Published by Carnegie Publishing Ltd., 18 Maynard Street, Preston, Lancashire, PR1 2AL.
Typeset in Times and Delphin by Carnegie Publishing Ltd.
Printed and bound in the UK by the Bath Press, Bath.

British Library Cataloguing-in-Publication Data
A CIP catalogue record for this book is available from the British Library.

ISBN 0-948789-79-4

Acknowledgements

Stephen Sartin, for expert advice, correction of errors and enthusiastic encouragement, and for providing photographs of Preston's town seals.

Pete Vickers and Norman Proctor, for valuable additional historical detail.

John Haslett, for use of his collection of articles on Private McCaffery.

Chris Pollington, for the musical scores.

Judith Flint, for special research at the Madden Collection.

Harry Walker and Neville Bridge of the Guild Office, for support.

Dave Byrnes, for some strategic advice right at the start.

Terence Shaw, Ann Dennison and Judith Wilson of the Harris Library, for help, tolerance and photocopying above and beyond the call of duty.

Brian and Angela Tatham, for putting up with us at the Eagle and Child at Wharles.

Carnegie Publishing, for producing this book.

The people of Preston through the ages, for making it easily interesting enough to justify this book.

Foreword

It surely is more than coincidence would allow, that Preston or 'Prestune', as it was spelt in the Domesday Book is a phonetic contraction of *Portus Sistuntiorum*, a name given by the Romans to a port apparently used by the Setantii tribe, and which is known to have existed somewhere in or around the Ribble Estuary in those remote times. This intriguing observation, hitherto overlooked, suggests that the origin of the name is Roman, and not the mediaeval 'Priest Town' which it has always been held to be. If the supposition is correct, then a thousand years can be added to the town's illustrious history.

Illustrious? Yes, because on so many occasions Preston has played a central rôle in events which have changed the course of history in the country itself. And here in the *Old Lamb and Flag*, with its carefully researched interpretations of the songs and ballads sung in the town long ago, that rôle has perhaps been more graphically and convincingly realised than in other weightier tomes of the past. It is a souvenir of souvenirs of Preston Guild 1992, which will be appreciated long after the event itself has faded into history.

And to those of you in the future lucky enough to find this book complete with its tape or CD, take the recording to your local museum, where they may be able to find you a compact disc player or cassette recorder in working order. I promise you, it will be well worth the effort . . . and they will also be able to direct you to the site of the Guild Hall where the show was first performed. They may even tell you, 'that old book of yours . . . *Portus Sistuntiorum* . . . yes, actually, it was right!'.

Stephen Sartin, 1992.

Introduction

The idea came, as so many good ones do, during a gentle evening of real-ale consumption. The time was August 1988, the place the Eagle and Child at Wharles, and the object of the exercise was very clearly to put the world to rights. The conversation strayed on to Preston Guild. 1992 was fast approaching and we pondered loudly that, while the 1972 Preston Guild had been a fabulous experience both of us having participated with Garstang Morris Men the relevance of most of the musical entertainment to Preston was, at best, minimal.

'The classical programme will be nice enough,' we said. 'And Liverpool Phil does actually visit us in non-Guild years, but the *music* won't be anything to do with Preston. Then there'll be a musical it's got to be popular, so it won't be a new production and certainly won't have any relevance to Preston they'll probably use *Oklahoma!*'

'And what about the folk song side of things,' we grumbled. 'They'll just import some big names from Liverpool or London, they'll sing the songs they'd sing anywhere else at any other time, the audience will sing choruses they could sing any other time, and while it might be a memorable evening, *Guild-memorable* it certainly won't be.'

We paused to refill our glasses and ponder on the incongruities of life. Then we mused on the fact that the pair of us had lived in Preston for over twenty years, had specialised in researching and singing popular songs from the earliest times to the present, had made about twelve albums between us, and had ready access to recording studios, record companies and fellow performers.

The pondering became deeper and quieter, and while no-one ever *did* shout 'Let's do the show right here!', that evening, by the time we were turfed out, we knew what had to be done, and who had to do it. We were going to write a show, record it on tape and CD and produce a book with the songs plus a short, readable history of the town and the show was to be aimed at the Charter Theatre during Guild Week. Not a bad evening's thought!

Once we had decided on the general format of the show we both knew that we had some serious research to do. We were sure that we could find appropriate songs and music but our knowledge of the history of the town was pretty sketchy after all, we were foreigners, so to speak. We knew that there was this thing called the 'Guild', we knew that there had been a battle here and that as a leading cotton town it had played a part in the Industrial Revolution; we even knew about 'Teetotallers' and the bullet holes in the Public Hall (although we weren't sure if the two facts were connected). In other words, we were about average on local history.

Twenty years of experience in traditional music meant that we knew where to find the songs. Prior to the nineteenth century we could rely on ballad collections to provide us with the 'hit of the day' appropriate to our tale. After 1800 we could also pick from ballads published by John Harkness, Preston's own song publisher for a large part of the last century; the collection of ballad sheets is available to view in the Harris Library at Preston. These are songs which were actually sung and enjoyed in the town itself. Nonetheless, there were quite a few problems making sure we had the right tune for the right words.

As for the history, it did not take too many hours head-down in the Reference Library for us to realise that the town can boast a saga of triumph and tragedy that can rival any of its better-known counterparts in the British Isles and, indeed, Europe.

From the Reformation onwards, through the turmoil of the Civil War and the Jacobite Rebellions, to the bitter social struggles of the nineteenth-century reformers and factory workers, Preston has always stood in the centre of the stage, very often under the main spotlight. It saw one of the most crucial battles of the Civil War in 1648, the last battle on English soil in 1715, the last occurrence of civilian deaths at the hands of the military in 1842, the first concerted industrial action (the Lock-Out) in 1853 . . . and many more firsts and lasts. All of these events were well documented by local commentators whose dry observations provide a far more vivid picture than more conventional history books.

Why does all this rumbustious history not enjoy a higher profile? Who knows? We believe Preston deserves it, so this is our contribution. We hope you enjoy the result.

PART I

From Lancashire of lusty blood . . .

OUR STORY begins on the banks of the Ribble in the remoteness of time. Here dwelt the proud and warlike Celtic tribe, the Setantii. Here also a town, Portus Sistuntiorum, was mentioned in the Roman itineraries, and it is not impossible that 'Preston' actually derives from the shortening of that name.

A more conventional explanation, however, is that Wilfrid (a bishop, later a saint) set up a small priory near the Ribble's lowest ford, and that this 'Priest's Town' was Preston's ancestor. What is certain is that the lamb, Wilfrid's banner, has become the town's symbol in the old Lamb and Flag. After the defeat of the Britons by Adelfrid at Chester in 613 AD the area fell under the influence of the Saxon kingdoms of Northumbria and Mercia, and Preston became a small but flourishing Saxon town. Preston saw the defeat of the Danes in 937 at the great battle of Brunanburgh fought 'at the pass of the Ribble' and the great Cuerdale hoard of 10,000 coins and silver bullion found on the Ribble banks may well be a relic of this battle.

In 1086 the Domesday Book mentions that the chief place in the Hundred of Amounderness (modern Fylde) was called Preston. The Domesday Book tells little and that was because there was little to tell. Lancashire in general and Preston in particular 'had its back to the rest of the known world and its face only to Wales, Ireland and the great ocean'. Preston looked into marshland to the south and north; eastwards lay a narrow plain leading to a rough and dangerous interior. True, anyone who *was* going south or north along the west side of Britain did go through Preston but such hardy souls were few and far between.

One who did pass through was William the Conqueror, in 1072. After the failure of a rebellion by the Earls Edwin and Morcar he was determined to teach the area a lesson and burned it. The town recovered rapidly and grew to become a borough. This may have been as early as the first year of the reign of Henry I, for most of the ancient code of Preston 'law', that document called the Custumal, contains references to trial by ordeal and the payment of Danegeld both of which were things of the past by the time that what is said to be the first recorded Preston Charter was granted by Henry II in 1179.

The Charter gave the town the right to have a 'Guild Merchant with all its liberties and free customs'. This meant that the well-to-do

Continued on page 4

Preston in the Domesday Book

301 d   *AGEMVNDRENESSE.*

In *PRESTVNE*, comes Tosti . vi . car ad gld . Ibi ptin he træ.

Estun . Lea . Saleuuic . Clistun . Neutune . Frecheltun . Rigbi.

Chicheham . Treueles . Westbi . Pluntun . Widetun . Pres . Wartun,

Lidun . Meretun . Latun . Staininghe . Carlentun . Bifcopham.

Rushale . Brune . Torentun . Poltun . Singletun . Greneholf.

Eglestun . alia Egleftun . Edelesuuic . Inscip . Sorbi . Aschebi.

Michelefcherche . Catrehala . Clactune . Neuhufe . Pluntun.

Broctun . Witingheham . Bartun . Gufanfarghe . Halctun.

Trelefelt . Watelei . Chipinden . Actun . Fifcuic . Grimefarge.

Ribelcastre . Bileuurde . Suenefat . Fortune . Crimeles . Che

reftanc . Rodeclif . alia Rodeclif . tcia Rodeclif . Hameltune.

Stalmine . Preffouede . Midehope.

Oms hæ uille iacent ad Preftune . 7 iii . ecclæ . Ex his . xvi.

a paucis incolunt . fƷ quot fint habitantes ignoratur.

Reliqua funt wafta . Rog pict habuit.

In **PRESTON**, Earl Tosti, 6 c. taxable.

These lands belong there

ASHTON 2 c., LEA 1 c., SALWICK 1 c., CLIFTON 2 c., NEWTON 2 c., FRECKLETON 4 c., RIBBY 6 c., KIRKHAM 4 c., TREALES 2 c., WESTBY 2 c., (Field) PLUMPTON 2 c., WEETON 3 c., PREESE 2 c., WARTON 4 c., LYTHAM 2 c., MARTON 6 c., LAYTON 6 c., STAINING 6 c., CARLETON 4 c., BISPHAM 8 c., ROSSALL 2 c., BURN 2 c., THORNTON 6 c., POULTON (le Fylde) 2 c., SINGLETON 6 c., GREENHALGH 3 c., ECCLESTON 4 c., the other (Little) ECCLESTON 2 c., ELSWICK 3 c., INSKIP 2 c., SOWERBY 1 c., *ASCHEBI* 1 c., ST MICHAEL'S (on Wyre) 1 c., CATTERALL 2 c., CLAUGHTON 2 c., NEWSHAM 1 c., (Wood) PLUMPTON 5 c., BROUGHTON 1 c., WHITTINGHAM 2 c., BARTON 4 c., GOOSNARGH 1 c., HAIGHTON 1 c., THRELFALL 1c., WHEATLEY 1 c., CHIPPING 3 c., AIGHTON 1 c., FISHWICK 1 c., GRIMSARGH 2 c., RIBCHESTER 2 c., DILWORTH 2 c., SWAINSEAT 1 c., FORTON 1 c., CRIMBLES 1 c., GARSTANG 6 c., (Upper) RAWCLIFFE 3 c., HAMBLETON 2 c., STALMINE 4c., PREESALL 6 c., MYTHOP 1 c.

All these villages and 3 churches belong to Preston. 16 of them have a few inhabitants, but how many is not known. The rest are waste. Roger of Poitou had them.

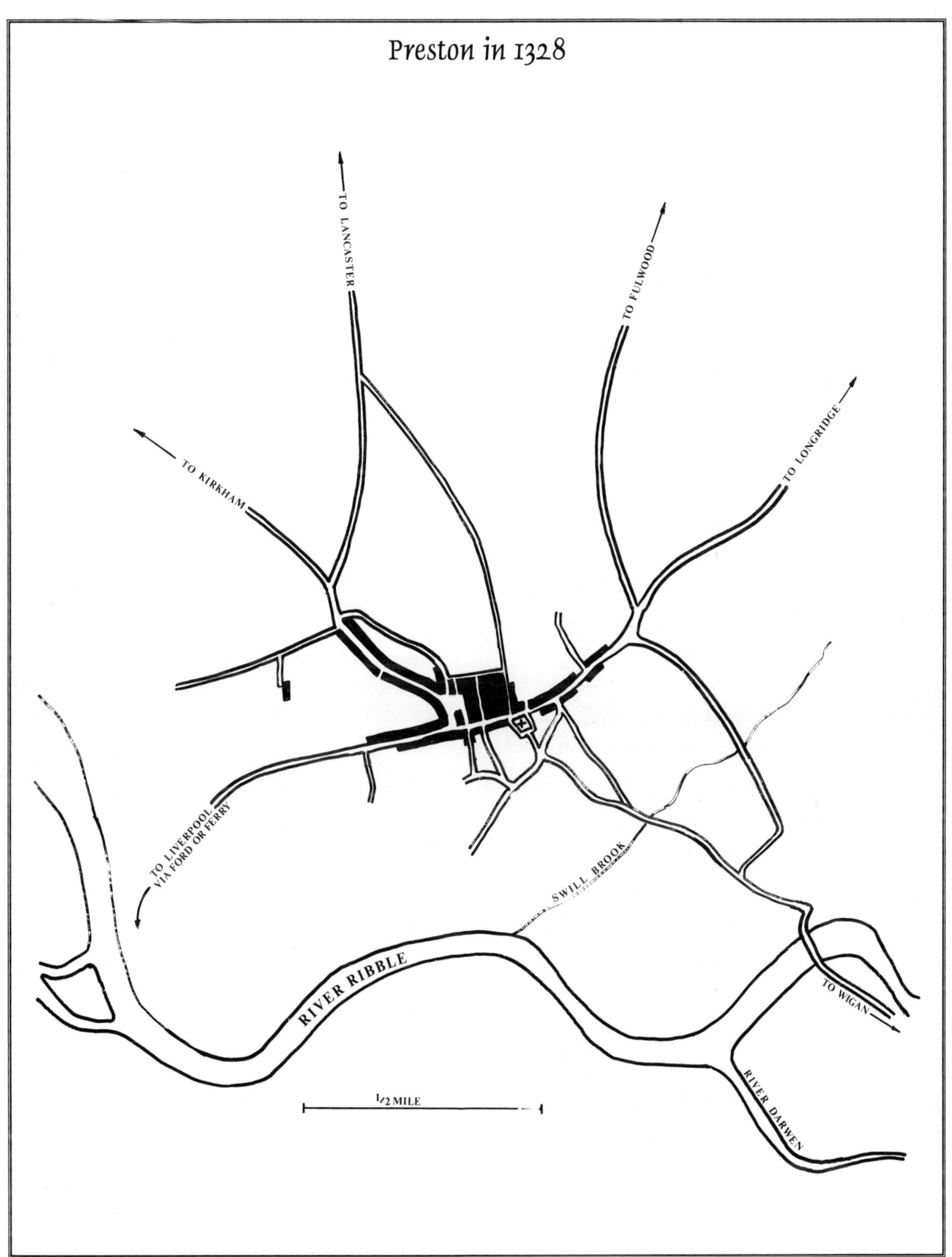
Preston in 1328
TO LANCASTER
TO FULWOOD
TO KIRKHAM
TO LONGRIDGE
TO LIVERPOOL, VIA FORD OR FERRY
SWILL BROOK
RIVER RIBBLE
TO WIGAN
RIVER DARWEN
1/2 MILE

The Wealth of Medieval Preston

In 1227 the records of tallage (taxation) on Lancashire towns[1] indicate payments of:

Lancaster	14 marks[2]	[£ 9.33]
Liverpool	11 marks, 7s. 8d.	[£ 7.71]
West Derby	7 marks, 4s. 4d.	[£ 4.88]
Preston	15 marks	[£10.00]

In 1332 the tax records for individuals in the various Lancashire towns are available[3] – and these, when added town by town, give:

Everton	13s. 4d.	[£ 0.67]
Salford	22s.	[£ 1.10]
Lytham	23s.	[£ 1.15]
Manchester	46s.	[£ 2.30]
West Derby	46s. 8d.	[£ 2.33]
Liverpool	47s.[4]	[£ 2.35]
Preston	53s. 4d.	[£ 2.67]

The picture clearly painted by both these records is of a Preston pre-eminent in wealth in Lancashire for much of the Middle Ages.

1. Hardwick, *History*, p. 353.
2. A mark was two-thirds of a pound – thus 13s. 4d., or 67p.
3. 'Exchequer Lay Subsidy Roll', Lancashire and Cheshire Records Society, 11, 48.31.
4. This is the total given in the 1332 book – the individual entries only add up to 46s, but Liverpool clearly got away with the extra shilling!

inhabitants of Preston (or 'burgesses') had exclusive control of anything sold in Preston and could also sell their own goods anywhere in the area that did *not* have such a charter. For this privilege the burgesses paid money into their association, or Guild, and the Guild in turn paid each new monarch a handsome sum for a new charter to renew the borough's privileges.

Most of the funds for these charters were raised periodically at a Guild Merchant, where all existing and new burgesses would pay a toll to affirm their membership of the Guild.

Preston was just getting round to one of these in 1323 when some unwelcome visitors trekked into the town from the north. It was the Scots army, led by Robert the Bruce. What was good enough for William the Conqueror was good enough for Bruce, so Preston was once again burned to the ground. However, such was the resilience of the townsfolk that only five years later in 1328 Aubrey, son of Robert, Mayor of Preston, held a Guild Court and those proceedings declared that a 'Guild Merchant shall be held every 20 years end, or earlier if need be'. We will see that it took 214 years before Preston started to obey its own rule.

By 1343 Preston was the richest of the Lancashire boroughs, but its joy was to be short-lived. Six years later in 1349 the Black Death Plague, which had been raging on the continent for several years, finally reached the town. Between September 8th 1349 and January 11th 1350, deaths numbered 3,000 in Preston alone, and 13,180 in the ten surrounding parishes.

Harvests were left to rot. The fields remained

Tuba Galicis

14th-century dance tune.

unploughed because there was nobody left to attend to them. As many people left the town to escape the plague as those that remained to die of it. Fifty-one years were to pass before another Guild Merchant was held in 1397.

In this year William Ergham presided over a Guild which already had trade companies well-developed. These were bodies by which each trade regulated standards, set prices and made sure no outsiders encroached on their territory. Those listed at the 1397 Guild Merchant include butchers, braziers, clock-makers, coopers, cordwainers, cow-leeches, flax-dressers, goldsmiths, grocers, haberdashers, innkeepers, joiners, mercers, merchants, skinners, saddlers, tailors and tanners.

In 1405 Prince Hal had passed through Preston. He succeeded to the throne in 1413 and granted the town its charter the following year. Preston's burgesses decided on a public declaration of loyalty to the House of Lanc-aster and held the Guild on 20th May 1415. Little did they know that before the year was out their loyalty would be put to the test. The king called the country to arms against France and many men fought with the Preston contingent at the battle of Agincourt on 25th October.

The Wars of the Roses raged for thirty years from 1455, as the ducal clans of Lancaster and York battled for the throne. To judge by the fervour generated these days at Old Trafford and Headingley, you would have thought that Lancashire in general and Preston in particular had great tales to tell. Not a bit of it! The forces of Lancashire were raised all right, and prot-estations of loyalty were made, but the *real* aim was to keep this unwanted dynastic strug-gle *out* of Lancashire while making sure we were on the winning side by the time it was won. This was successfully managed, and not a single battle of any consequence was fought in Lancashire.

The only bit of excitement occurred two years after Henry Tudor had defeated Richard III at Bosworth Field and declared the wars over. In June 1487 Lambert Simnel, given out

The Black Death In Preston

The Black Death struck Preston suddenly in 1349, with many people dying before being able to make out a will — and it is to this that we owe what detail we possess of the plague in the town.

The church derived considerable income from those dying intestate, and this money was collected by the Dean of Amounderness, one Adam de Kirkham. This should have been passed on up the ecclesiastical ladder to the Dean of Richmond; in the event the Dean was dissatisfied with the amount being forwarded, sued de Kirkham, and the parchment recording his claims survives in the Public Record Office.[1] The account, in Old French, uses very round numbers and clearly does not attempt to be accurate, but even so it paints a terrible picture of sudden death throughout Amounderness in general and Preston in particular.

The death toll of 3,000 in Preston probably represented over half the population, and is on a similar scale to the numbers quoted for parishes round about. In eleven parishes over 13,000 are quoted as dying between 8th September 1349 and 11th January 1350. The benefices of nine of eleven parishes were made vacant (presumably by the death of the priest) during this period, three of them twice.

Incidentally, the sum claimed by the Archdeacon was £48.50 — a vast amount at the time and one which underlines the view of a prosperous community overtaken by catastrophe.

1. A. G. Little, *English Historical Review* V.524.
Illustration: Euing Ballads, No. 371.

Continued on page 11

The Doleful Dance and Song of Death

Words: Black-letter ballad reprinted PMOT 85
Tune: *The shaking of the sheets*, ibid.

Can you dance the shaking of the sheets,
A dance that everyone must do?
Can you trim it up with dainty sweets,
And everything that 'longs thereto?
Make ready then your winding sheet
And see how ye can bestir your feet,
For Death is the man that all must meet. (x 2)

Bring away the beggar and the king
And every man in his degree;
Bring away the old and the youngest thing
Come all to death and follow me;
The courtier with his lofty looks,
The lawyer with his learned books,
The banker with his baiting hooks. (x 2)

Think you I dare not come to schools
Where all the cunning clerks are most?
Take I not away both wives and fools
And am I not on every coast?
Assure yourselves no creature can
Make Death afraid of any man,
Or know my coming, where or when, (x 2)

For I can quickly cool you all.
Or hot or stout soever you be;
Both high or low, both great and small
I nought do fear your high degree;
The lady fair, the beldams old,
The champions stout, the soldier bold
Must all with me to earthly mould. (x 2)

Therefore take time while it is lent
Prepare with me yourselves to dance;
Forget me not, your lives lament,
I come oft-times by sudden chance.
Be ready, therefore, watch and pray,
That when my minstrel pipe doth play,
You may to heaven dance the way. (x 2)

The tune is frequently mentioned and printed in publications from 1560 to the present day. It was used both as a country dance tune and for ballads, and was clearly already old and familiar by the mid-1500s. The words paint a matter-of-fact yet chilling picture of the supremacy of death – and well mirror the helplessness of a community visited by a plague such as the Black Death.

Agincourt Carol

Words 'From a manuscript copy in the Pepys collection,'
reprinted PRAEP 2 29.
Tune: Ibid, reprinted PMOT 39.

Our King went forth to Normandy
With grace and might of chivalry
And God for him wrought marvellously
Wherefore England may call and cry,
Deo gratias!

He set a siege the truth to say
To Harfleur town with royal array
Which town he won and made a fray
Which France shall rue till Domesday,
Deo gratias!

Then went our King with all his host
Through France, for all the French's boast
He spared for dread of least nor most
Until he came to Agincourt coast,
Deo gratias!

Then went him forth our King comely
At Agincourt field he fought manly
Through grace of God most marvellously
He had both field and victory,
Deo gratias!

Almighty God, then keep our King
His people and all his well-being
And them grace without ending
Then we may call and gladly sing,
Deo gratias!

The impact of the victory at Agincourt on October 25th 1415 is well illustrated by the fact that at least three more or less contemporary ballads survive on the subject. *Agincourt or the English Bowmens Glory* is quoted in Heywood's *King Edward IV*, and begins, 'Agincourt! Agincourt! Know ye not Agincourt? Where the English slew or hurt all the French foemen?'. *The Battayle of Aginkourte* was an early minstrel piece and is printed in HEP, 2 257. *Henry V's Conquest of France* has been much reprinted and survived in traditional form into the present century; it is reprinted in TTCB 3 127. The present song is the very stuff of which legends are made, and it is easy to see why many Preston lads were swept into Henry's French adventures.

The Battle Of Flodden

9th September 1513

That day Sir Edward Stanley stout
For martial skill clear without match
Of Lathom House by line came out
Whose blood will never turn their back
All Lancashire will live and die.

From Lancashire of lusty blood
A thousand soldiers stiff in fight
The lusty Stanley stout can lead
A stock of striplings strong of heart
Brought up from babes with beef and bread.

From Poulton to Preston Proud with pikes
They with the Stanley out forth went
From Pemberton and Pilling Dykes
For battle billmen bold were bent
With lusty lads, liver and light.

Excerpt from *Flodden Field*, 1513 (Harlean Ms, coll 3526) reprinted in
Ballads and Songs of Lancashire, John Harland, 1865.

When Henry VIII invaded France in 1513, the terms of the 'Auld Alliance' between Scotland and France obliged the Scots King James to support the French. Foolishly, as it turned out, he decided to do this by invading northern England, hoping to bring Henry scurrying back from France.

Around 40,000 men crossed the border on 22nd August 1513, but after desertions and dissent rather less than 30,000 assembled on the battlefield outside Branxton in Northumberland on 9th September. The army that opposed them was, in the absence of England's main force in France, a cross section of northern society, with the local lords and gentry bringing along the yeomen and peasants from their estates. They were largely not professional soldiers, but well accustomed to bearing arms and there were many archers. The army probably totalled around 26,000.

In the manner of the times, challenge had been given (by the English) and accepted, and James had taken up a strong defensive position on Flodden Hill. Knowing that an attack on this position would have little chance, Surrey, the English commander, marched his army round the Scottish flank and confronted the Scots from the north. The Scots army about-faced and took up a position one mile north on Branxton Hill.

The battle opened with a cannonade at around 4.00pm, but very little damage was done. The English barrage did, however, unnerve the borderers who, hating to be shot at while standing still, abandoned their defensive position and charged down the hill, taking with them Huntley's Highlanders. Though the English right wing was hard pressed, the Scots advance was eventually halted.

Now, possibly thinking the attack had turned the

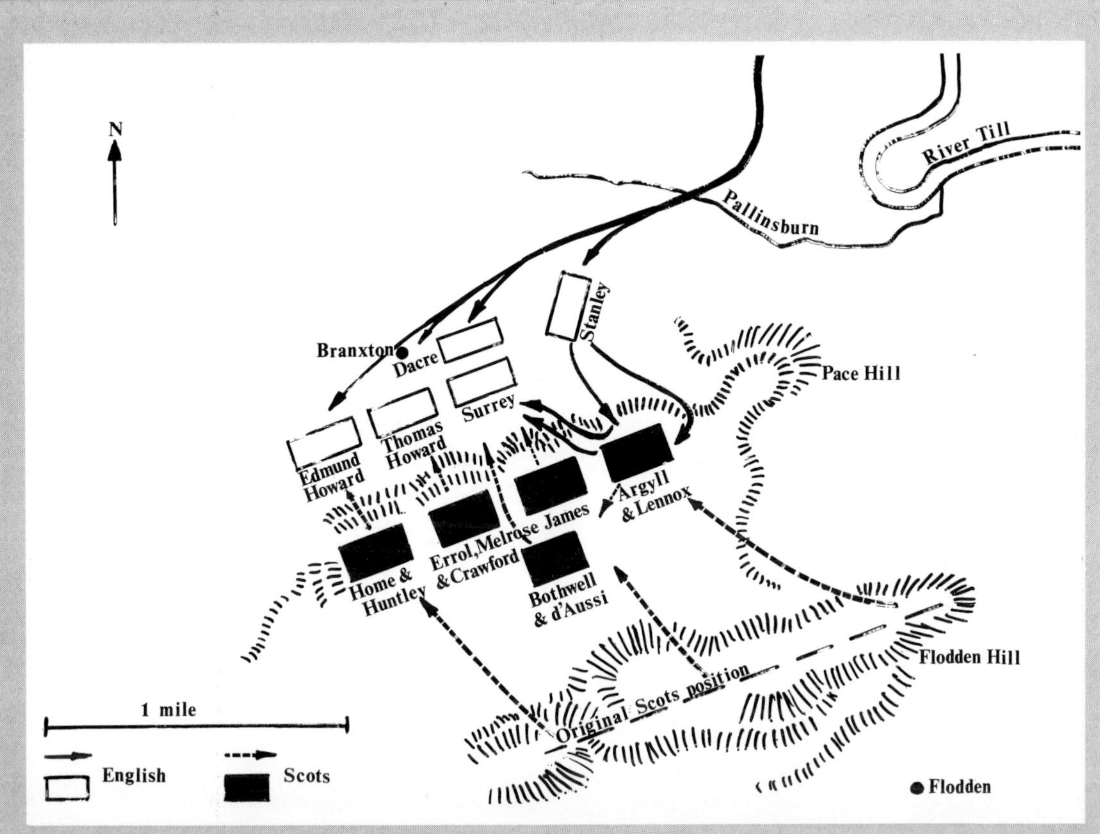

English flank, James ordered the rest of the Scottish army to advance. This meant leaving their prepared position and slithering down a wet, grassy hillside, across a boggy area and then slightly uphill into the English ranks. At this stage the Scots' technology failed them. They had been introduced to the heavy two-handed long pike by the French, but had not been sufficiently trained in its use, and once they were slowed down by the rising ground, the English bills chopped the pikes into uselessness.

The Highlanders on the Scots right flank were not yet engaged, and the Cheshire and Lancashire contingent under Lord Stanley, arriving last on the battlefield (as the English left wing) engaged the Scots on both front and flank, routed them and drove them from the field. Stanley then re-formed his men and charged down the hill at the Scots right flank. The Scots had no escape and, though they fought on without hope, by nightfall a proud army had simply ceased to exist.

Among over 5,000 killed were many of the Scots nobles, and their king. A generation had been destroyed, and the flowers of the forest were to take many generations to regain their vigour.

Flodden Field

Words: Traditional, printed AMSS 1 45.
Tune: 1. Variant on (2), Gregg Butler (1977).
2. *Flowers of the Forest,* traditional.

From Spey to the border was peace and good order
The sway of our monarch was mild as the May
Peace he adored which the English abhorred
Our marches they plunder, our wardens they slay.

'Gainst Louis our ally their Henry did sally
Though James but in vain did his herald advance
Renouncing alliance and announcing defiance
Of Soudrons if longer abiding in France.

England's invasion it was our persuasion
To make restitution for their cruelty
But oh, fatal Flodden, there came the woe down,
And our royal nation was brought to decay.

The flowers of the nation were brought to their station
With valiant inclination their banners to display
To Burrow-muir resorting their right for supporting
And there rendezvousing encamped they lay.

The English advanced to where they were stanced.
Half-intrenched by nature the field it so lay
To fight the English fearing and shamed their retiring
But alas unperceived was their subtlety.

Our Highland battalion so forward and valiant
They broke from the ranks and they rushed on to slay
With hacking and slashing and broadswords a-dashing
Through the front of the English they cut a full sway.

But alas to their ruin, an ambush pursuing,
They were surrounded by numbers too high.
The Merse men and Forest they suffered the sorest
Upon the left wing was enclosed the same way.

Our men into parties, the battle into quarters,
Upon our main body their marksmen did play.
The spearmen were surrounded and all was confounded
The fatal devastation of that woeful day.

Our nobles all ensnared, our king he was not spared
For of that fate he shared for he would not run away.
The whole were intercepted that very few escaped
The fatal conflagration of that woeful day.

I've heard them lilting at our ewe-milking
Lassies a-lilting before break of day
But now there's a moaning on ilka green loaming
Since our braw foresters are a' wed away.

At buchts in the morning nae blithe lads are scorning
The lassies are lonely and dowy and wae,
Nae laughing, nae gabbing, but sighing and sobbing
Each one lifts her leglen and hies her away.

A dool for the order sent our lads to the border
The English for once by guile won the day
The flowers of the forest that aye shone the foremost
The pride of our land lies as cold as the clay

I've seen the morning with gold the hills adorning
And proud tempests storming before the midday
I have seen Tweed's silver streams shining in the
    sunny beams
Grow drumly and dark as it flows on its way.

I've heard them lilting at our ewe-milking
Lassies a-lilting before the break of day
But now there's a moaning on ilka green loaming
The Flowers of the Forest are all wed away.

The second part of this ballad is one of the most famous Scottish songs, but the narrative which precedes it is much more rarely heard, and a quicker variant of the tune is used here. That the battle was significant to both sides is evidenced by a stirring English song of the same title, commencing 'King Jamie hath made a vow, keep it well if he may!' This is printed, for example, in BES, 304.

to be Edward, Earl of Warwick, son of the Duke of Clarence, landed at Peel Island (in Furness) and marched south through Lancashire. Preston and the other Lancashire towns weighed matters carefully, decided the odds were by no means good enough, were polite but unenthusiastic, and said a quiet 'I told you so' when Simnel and his supporters came to an untimely end on the battlefield at Stoke.

Henry Tudor was followed by his son Henry VIII. By 1513 his foreign policy was leading England and France inexorably to war. The 'Auld Alliance' between France and Scotland saw its opportunity and the Scots king James IV began to see himself as king of England. He had agreed to advance into England should Henry invade France, and when in June the English king crossed the channel at the head of a large English army, James honoured his pledge at the head of 40,000 men.

The defence of the north of England had been entrusted to the Earl of Surrey, a man of 70 who had fought for Richard III at Bosworth! He arrived with his army at Alnwick on 3rd September, where he was joined by his eldest son Thomas Howard, the Lord Admiral, with soldiers from his fleet. He had raised a militia of 26,000 men, mainly drawn from the north of England. In particular, one Sir Edward Stanley commanded 3,000 men from Cheshire and Lancashire with a contingent of pikemen from Preston whose exploits justly gave them a place in ballad literature, for the success of Stanley's forces on the left wing was decisive. (The tradition of the devastating Prestonian left wing in Anglo-Scots confrontations was to be developed further in modern times by footballer Tom Finney.)

The battle was fought on the 9th September at Flodden, near Branxton in Northumberland, and the songs of the time echo the effect on Scotland of a generation lost.

This distant battle was to have a significant effect on the tale of Preston. Firstly, Scots invaders never again used the eastern route (presumably it was not good for the morale of the troops to pass Flodden at the start of an invasion); henceforth they always used the western route which led inexorably to the town on the Ribble bridge. Secondly, it confirmed the Stanley family as the area's most powerful barons, and their influence on the history of the town commences here.

When Henry broke with the Catholic Church the Stanleys kept allegiance to him, strength-

Continued on page 14

The Plague in Preston, 1630–1631

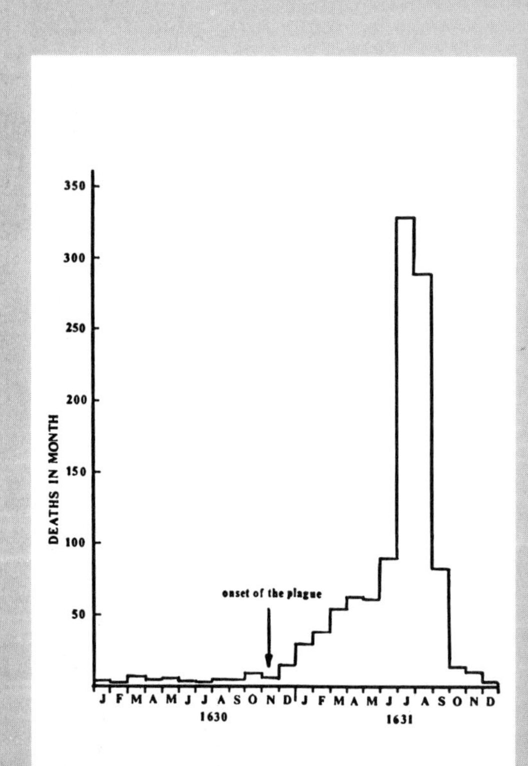

The records for Preston Parish Church[1] for January to October 1630 reveal 54 deaths, sixteen marriages and 76 christenings – a picture of a stable, even growing, community of some 3–4,000.

In November 1630 is the stark entry: 'Here beginneth the visit of almighty God the Plague', and the following twelve months were to yield 1,078 deaths, with only seven marriages and 37 christenings. 331 died in the month of July 1631 alone.

Unlike the Black Death, which seems to have struck Lancashire fairly uniformly, the plague in 1631 was concentrated in Preston. The whole county was charged with the weekly sum of £60 towards Preston's relief. In the last week of April 1631, 1,390 people received various sums between ninepence and one shilling (4–5p) from this money, and presumably used it to buy fuel and provisions which had been directed to be brought to 'some convenient place near to the town'.

By 16th August 1631 the happy community of less than twelve months before had been reduced by death and flight to only 887 people in a stunned and isolated town. By the end of October 1631 the plague departed as quickly as it had come, and it was time for the remaining inhabitants once more to pick up the threads of Preston's existence.

1. Smith, *Records of Preston Parish Church.*

Fortune my Foe

Words: Modified (Gregg Butler, 1991) from anon copy in BB, 961.
Tune: Widely printed from *circa* 1590, for example FVB 1 254,
and reprinted PMOT 162.

Fortune my foe, why dost thou frown on me?
And will thy favours never better be?
Wilt thou, I say, forever breed my pain
And wilt thou not restore my joys again?

No man alive can fortune's spite withstand,
When mighty dread afflicts this sorry land.
In midst of mirth she bringeth bitter moan
And woe to we that have her hatred known.

In vain we sigh; in vain we wail and weep.
In vain by night our torchlight vigil keep.
In vain we pray deliverance to receive
But still midst death and suffering we grieve.

This tune was widely known and used from before 1600 until the end of the seventeenth century. Its solemn tones were ideal for any sad subject, and were used for countless hanging ballads, stories of destruction, of deformed births and outlandish creatures, of brushes with the devil, and of natural disasters – including death through plague and pestilence. If there were voices left to sing in Preston in 1631, then the tune of *Fortune my Foe* cannot have been far from their thoughts or lips.

ening their position further. However, in the north, and especially the North West, there were many who could not square politics against religion. Many paid the ultimate penalty for a refusal to accept the new Church of England. In 1536 the Pilgrimage of Grace commenced in Yorkshire; a rising mainly in reaction to Henry's destruction of the Catholic monasteries and reallocation of their wealth into the state (i.e. his own) coffers. Edward Stanley, now titled Earl of Derby, mustered 8,000 men at Preston which dissuaded any similar rebellion in central Lancashire. However, many in the area continued to adhere to the old religion openly or in secret, and not a few chose actively to resist the new order. Many paid with their lives since, in those troubled times, such action was simply equated with treason.

As for the Guilds, following 1415 there were others in 1459 and 1500, but it was only after the 1542 Guild that the intention to hold the Guild regularly was taken seriously. From then on they were celebrated every twenty years, except in 1942 when the Second World War led to a postponement for ten years. The Tudor years passed quietly for Preston, with gradually increasing prosperity which enabled the town to send members to Parliament after 1529 this having been abandoned in 1331 as too expensive! In particular, the Charter of Elizabeth I in 1566 gave in considerable detail the rules by which the borough was to be governed not that the good folk of Preston always took the town rules too seriously. Throughout the sixteenth century Preston was entertained by a continuing wrangle on how, when and by whom the mayor should be elected. This made modern local government squabbles seem positively anaemic, with intimidation on a grand scale, people fleeing the Moot Hall in fear of their lives, and with rustling, affray and murder between the protagonists. The hostilities seem to have been resolved at the end of Elizabeth's reign.

At her death the Stuart King, James VI of Scotland, was invited to London to unite the crowns of Scotland and England. He made a well-publicised visit to Preston in 1617, when he was banqueted at the Guild Hall and knighted the loin of beef at nearby Hoghton Towers. Preston was then happy to be out of the limelight once again.

Proud Preston's peace was undisturbed until on 10th November 1630 the parish register gained the entry 'Here beginneth the visitation of Almighty God the Plague'. This raged for a year and killed 1,100 people in the town. At its height, died in the two months of July and August 1631, 599 died. The whole of Lancashire was taxed to give help, but by August 16th only 887 were left alive in Preston. As always, Preston recovered, but it was many years before the scars of 1630 were forgotten and then they were soon to be replaced by scars of a different sort. . .

PART II

'When cannons are roaring ...'

JAMES' SON, Charles I, began to forfeit the loyalty of many of his subjects, not only for his autocratic behaviour, but also for suspected Catholic sympathies under the influence of his French wife.

The Civil War represented a turning point for Preston. Having spent over half a millennium as a backwater, scarcely affecting or affected by the tides of history, Preston was at the dawn of two hundred years during which the mainstream of history would come to call more than once, usually without knocking!

Guild year of 1642, which coincided with the outbreak of the Civil War, saw Preston assume a pivotal rôle as *the* great strategic town, commanding as it did the crucial north-south route up the west coast and also the pass into Yorkshire via the Ribble Valley and Skipton.

In Civil War terms Preston was a finely-drawn marginal. The great family of Stanley was on the side of the king, and its head, James Stanley, 7th Earl of Derby, was the leading Royalist of Lancashire and Cheshire. Sir Gilbert Hoghton was also prominent for the king, but both the Stanley and Hoghton families had Parliamentary adherents, and this confusion of relationships and divided loyal-ties was typical of the turmoil found nearly everywhere at the time. Even before hostilities had commenced Stanley had called a 'Randez-vous' at Preston on 20th June 1642 to hear two declarations from the king and his reply to a petition from Lancashire. Various Parliamentarians tried to hinder this gathering, but fully 5,000 men assembled on Fulwood Moor close to the town and gave a 'shout for the king'. The influence of the Stanleys, plus the large Catholic population, who generally supported the king, kept an uneasy Royalist hold on the town at this stage, though both the Guild Mayor, Edmund Worden, and the town's M.P.s were for Parliament. Beneath the surface, however, was a great sense of loyalty to the town, and the first priority of very many of the townsfolk was to ensure that Preston unfailingly supported the winning side. This had worked admirably during the Wars of the Roses, and changing a winning formula has never been a strong part of Preston tradition.

On August 24th Charles raised his standard at Nottingham. One month later Stanley started the war in Lancashire with an attack on Manchester, which was held for Parliament. The siege failed; Parliament now had a secure foothold in Lancashire and Preston's chances

When Cannons Are Roaring

Words: Cantus, songs and Fancies', John Forbes (1662), reprinted SMRC 42.
Tune: ibid.

Hark, the alarum call, war-clouds a-thundering,
Foemen in wood and vale, through the towns
   plundering,
Then will the brave and true, to standard rallying,
Fight for their land and laws, rushing and sallying.

   Chorus:
   When cannons are roaring and bullets are flying
   He that would honour win must not fear dying

Soldiers with sword in hand, to the walls coming,
Horsemen about the streets riding and running,
Sentinels on the walls 'Arm, Arm' a-crying,
Petards against the ports, wildfire a-flying.

Trumpets on turret high, these are a-sounding,
Drums beating out aloud, echoes resounding.
Alarm bells in each place they are a-ringing,
Grappling hooks rope-tailed rise, to the walls
   clinging.

Captains in open field on their foes rushing,
Musketeers' bullets wild down those foes cutting,
Now soon at push of pike, horses uprearing,
Standards still held aloft through smoke appearing.

The tune for this song had been in existence from at least 1624, and the song itself was referred to from 1637. It was popular in the Civil War period and is one of the 'blood and thunder' songs which are so well balanced by the many rather more thoughtful political and sociological songs written during the conflict.

The Contented

Words: Rearranged and slightly rewritten (Gregg Butler, 1986) after an
anonymous original printed MDC, 27.
Tune: Gregg Butler (1986).

So why should any man complain?
Or why disturb his heart and brain
At this new alteration?
Since that which has been done's no more
Than what has oft been done before
And that which will be done again
As long as there are ambitious men
Who strive for domination.

In this mad age there's nothing firm
All things have period and their turn
For rising and declining.
Without our help affairs of state
They pass at their ordained rate.
We watch but neither cheer nor frown
Which e'er side's up, we're always down.
There's no use for cheers or whining.

So still we commons must indeed
Be made a starveling hackney steed
For all in turns will ride us.
This side or that, no matter which,
For both do ride with spur and switch
Till soon we tire and then at last
We stumble and our riders cast
For they'll not feed nor guide us.

The lawyers must leave by their books
They and the clergy quite mistook
Thought crowns were gained by prating.
Tis not the black coat but the red
Has power to take and be the head
Nor is it psalms nor laws nor tears
But muskets and full bandoliers
Have power of legislating.

Such wit and valour, root all things,
They pull down and they set up kings.
We'll not presume to judge them
For that side's always right that's strong
And that that's beaten must be wrong.
We common folks books stay fast at home
And Heaven help the slack-brained mome
That law or scripture quotes from tome
Thinking with right to gain his own
He's from his living quickly thrown
And was but a fool to oppose them.

One of the more thoughtful and cynical Civil War songs. The common folk reasoned out fairly quickly that, whoever was going to win the Civil War, it wasn't going to be them!

of a quiet war were ended. In October an ardent Royalist, Adam Mort, was elected mayor, but as a Royalist Catholic surrounded by a Parliamentarian Council, he felt unable to discharge his duty and refused to take office. An improvement in Royalist fortunes finally persuaded him to relent and assume the title of Mayor. Indeed, the Royalists felt confident enough to reduce the Preston garrison.

On February 9th 1643, however, a force of 1,600 Parliamentarians marched from Manchester through Bolton and Blackburn and launched a sudden attack on Preston. A small number raised a diversion at the Penwortham fords, but the main attack came from the east at Church Street. Two hours of hand-to-hand fighting were enough to take the town for Parliament. Adam Mort, his son and several others were killed; many others were taken prisoner. Only three or four Parliamentarian soldiers died. As Mort had declared that he would fire the town rather than let it be taken by Parliament, it is unlikely that the bulk of Prestonians mourned his loss.

Edmund Worden was re-appointed mayor and Prestonians, who on the evening of February 8th had been staunchly Royalist, now found themselves to be staunchly Parliamentarian.

They remained Parliamentarian for just over a month. On the night of March 20th who should return but James Stanley, Earl of Derby, with over 4,000 men. Edmund Worden refused to surrender, but after only an hour's fighting against this vastly superior force the Parliamentarian defenders retreated. Preston was now again in Royalist hands.

Two weeks later Derby set out eastward from Preston up the Ribble Valley with his army to attack the Parliamentarians towards Blackburn. At Whalley he encountered a small Parliamentarian force under Colonel Shuttleworth. In spite of being greatly outnumbered, they defeated Derby and bundled him in disarray back down the valley and out into the Lancashire Plain. By giving him no opportunity to regroup they were able to capture Wigan, Warrington and Liverpool. Preston was the first to be recaptured (staunchly Parliamentarian yet again), and by the end of June 1643 only two isolated Royalist strongpoints remained in Lancashire: Lathom House (Derby's home and headquarters near Ormskirk), and Greenhalgh Castle near Garstang.

All was quiet till the following May of 1644. Prince Rupert and 15,000 Royalists heading for Yorkshire by way of the Ribble Valley marched into Preston without meeting any resistance. He was given an official reception, but responded by taking the Parliamentarian mayor and bailiffs captive along with him to Skipton. This underlines that, although Preston was always a 'Parliamentary/Royalist marginal', the governing body of the town tending to Parliament while the ordinary townsfolk shaded towards the king, the main imperative was Preston, hence unfailing support for the winning side.

From Skipton, the Royalist army marched to defeat at Marston Moor. This was the turning point of the war. Rupert, along with the tattered remains of his force, fled back down the Ribble Valley to Preston. From there Rupert sped into Cheshire while his army looted the Fylde, sneaked across the Ribble at Freckleton to avoid the Parliamentarians at Preston (once again), but were again defeated and scattered at Ormskirk. Liverpool fell to Parliament on 1st November 1644 and, after a year-long siege, Lathom House was captured in December 1645.

By 1648 the only effective power in the land was that of Oliver Cromwell's New Model Army, into whose hands the king had now fallen.

Charles began to intrigue with the Scots who, up to then, had stayed out of the English war. By promising to impose Presbyterianism on England he persuaded them to invade a war-weary nation on his behalf.

Led by the Duke of Hamilton, the Scots army

A Marching Song of the New Model Army

Words: Adapted and collated (Gregg Butler, 1985) from *Lesley's March to Scotland* and *Lesley's March to Longmarston Moor*, printed JROS, 4-7.
Tune: ibid.

March, march, army of saints
March in good order where culverin rattle
March, march, conscience of Parliament
Hold your faith fast in the height of the battle.
Scourges of heresy, popery's foemen,
Rough-mannered psalmists in God's name to fight,
Puritan tradesman and leveller yeoman,
Sustain ye by fervour by righteousness armour.

March, march, blest ragamuffins,
Sing as ye go the hymns of rejoicing,
March, march, justified ruffians,
Chosen of heaven to glory you're rising.
Humble, implacable, strong in your faith,
Marching, invincible, into God's grace,
Red-coated prophets, you New Model come
With the fire of the right to bring England to order.

March, march, army of saints,
Onward with psalms to the push of the pike now.
March, march, host of the righteous
To triumph or martyrdom – so 'tis your right now.
Rustic philosophers, farm theologians,
Mind-questing pamphleteers, to the ranks come,
City apprentice and Anglian yokel,
Unite with intention Gomorrah to level.

March, march, sharp-sworded midwives
Of God's new millennium born in its glory.
March, march, pike-staffed physicians
To purge England's ills and an end to outlawry.
Marching in ranks to the Gospel's command
Marching for Commonwealth, God and the land,
Red-coated prophets, you New Model come
With the fire of the right to bring England to order.

This song was brought together in response to repeated (and sometimes menacing!) requests from Sealed Knot gatherings for 'a good stirring song for the parliamentarian side'. The closest we could come was to adapt two contemporary songs used by the Scots, notably during their intervention in the Civil War at the Battle of Marston Moor. The song is therefore wholly contemporary with the Civil War – but has changed armies! The tune was very popular and persisted well into the last century, and is used for at least two songs in the Harkness Collection (1 48 and 2 37).

crossed the border on 8th July 1648. In Carlisle they were joined by English Royalists under Sir Marmaduke Langdale and their numbers swelled to well over 20,000. They marched south through Cumberland into Lancashire, unnopposed and confident.

Parliament had only 9,000 troops to face them, and these were in Yorkshire. However, these were New Model Army veterans and led by Cromwell himself. He raced eastward through Otley to Skipton and arrived at Gisburn on the evening of August 15th. Passing through Clitheroe on the 16th, he kept to the north of the Ribble and received updated reports on the situation at Stonyhurst. The first Scots troops had reached Preston, but the rest were strung out back past Lancaster. Langdale was camped on Ribbleton Moor near Eaves Brook on Preston's eastern edge, protecting their line of march.

The following day Cromwell's veterans hurled themselves at Langdale's troops on Ribbleton Moor. The Scots cavalry had already crossed the river and were proceeding to Wigan, while some of the infantry were actually crossing Walton bridge. The Scots left the English to fight it out. Few came to the aid of Langdale who, after the initial impact, made a fighting retreat from Ribbleton along the present Deepdale Road, Ribbleton Lane, Acregate Lane, Stanley Street, London Road, Frenchwood Avenue and through the Strawberry Gardens to the old bridge, which was taken 'at push of pike' in one of the most ferocious engagements of the entire war. Cromwell's army crossed the River Darwen, cutting the Royalists to pieces in their advance. The victory was commemorated by Milton in his *Ode to Oliver Cromwell*.

By the end of the day Cromwell had cut the Scots army in two and was firmly in control of the Ribble and Darwen bridges. There were 4,000 Scots and Royalist prisoners, with many more heading back north as quickly as they could. The Scots who had crossed the river were pursued to Wigan and, after losing 1,000

men in a battle at Winwick, the infantry surrendered at Warrington. The 3,000 remaining cavalry crossed the Mersey and did not finally surrender until August 22nd at Uttoxeter.

The hundreds of dead from the Ribbleton Moor battle were buried in a ditch (or 'sough' in the local dialect) and were soon forgotten. Over three hundred years later, contractors working on the Preston Bypass froze as excavators suddenly revealed masses of human bones. Only then did the full significance of the name of the nearby Killingsough Farm become evident.

Cromwell spent that night at the Unicorn Inn in Walton-le-Dale, giving thanks that this most serious threat to the Parliamentarian victory had been removed. That threat and the attendant loss of life could only be attributed to the machinations of the king.

As a result of the Battle of Preston the execution of Charles I was both inevitable and deserved – and as Charles had in his time both refused Preston a Charter *and* finished on the losing side, he was probably not deeply mourned in the town.

The next passage of troops through Preston was August 13th 1651. Once more the army was largely Scots, this time led by Charles II who had been proclaimed king in Scotland following the execution of his father in 1649. Charles had great hopes of popular support in the North West, but the people of Preston, numbed by eight years of the ebb and flow of warring factions, could raise little enthusiasm for his cause as he passed through the town. Stanley arrived to hold a 'randezvous' again the following week (which implies that the town was again fleetingly Royalist), but even his presence could not persuade the townsfolk to rise. Charles' army was shattered at Worcester on September 3rd. Charles escaped to France. Stanley was captured and beheaded in Bolton on October 15th.

Cromwell ruled the nation as Lord Protector for nearly ten years till his death. The post did

Continued on page 27

The Battle of Preston, 17th August 1648

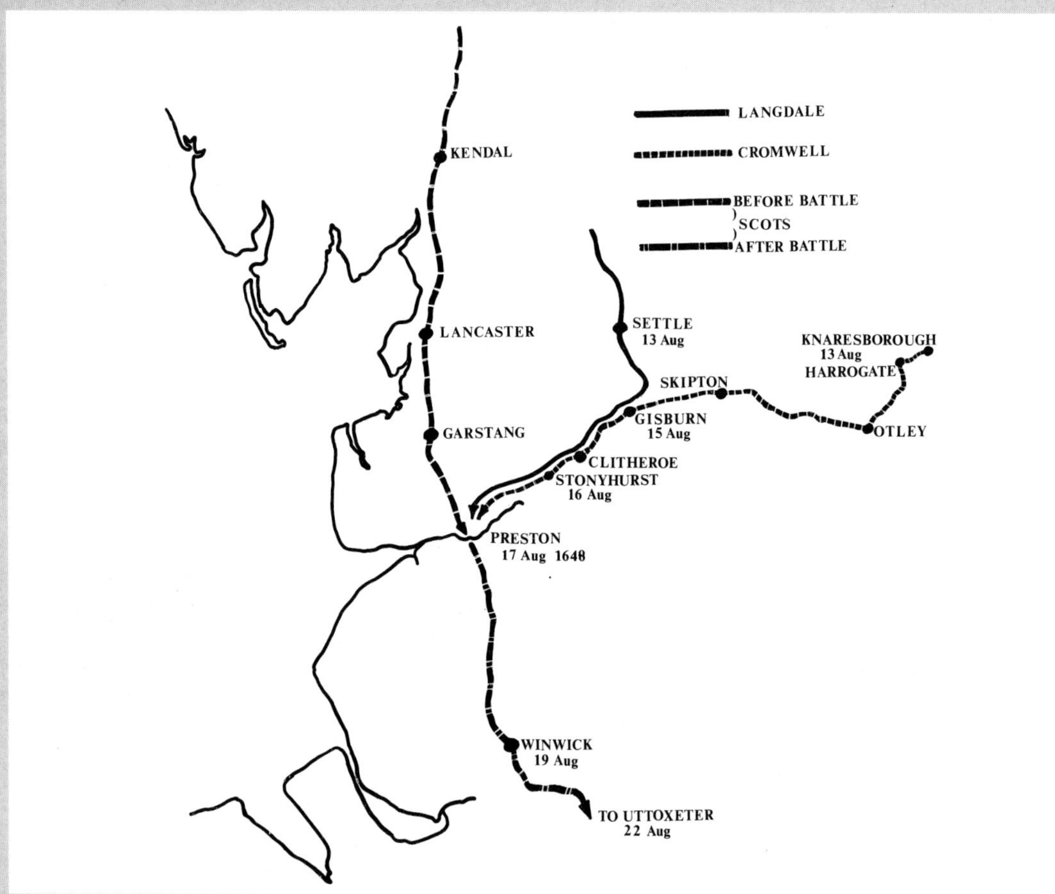

In 1648 Charles I, while imprisoned on the Isle of Wight, *de jure* by Parliament but very much *de facto* by the army, intrigued with the Scots and eventually entered into the 'Engagement' with them which, among other things, undertook to establish Presbyterianism in England for three years.

The army was the only real power in England at the time, a state of affairs which was abhorrent to many people, even those who were not primarily Royalist in their sympathies. The king became, almost by default, the 'cause' for many uprisings, such as those in the south-eastern counties, Wales, and part of the fleet, some of which were basically anti-army rather than pro-king. One such uprising was in the North of England, where the Royalists, under Sir Marmaduke Langdale, had occupied Carlisle. These were being shadowed by a small Parliamentarian force under Colonel Lambert, but on July 8th 1648 any thoughts that this would merely be a local skirmish had to be put aside.

On that day a Scots army under the Duke of Hamilton crossed the border to invade England, place Charles back on the throne, and have him carry out the 'Engagement'. Lambert retreated towards Yorkshire and help from Cromwell, while the

Scots waited for artillery and further reinforcements. It was not until 9th August that the Scots entered Lancashire. Three thousand veterans from Ulster under Sir George Munroe had joined at Kendal, bringing the total of the Scots and Royalist army to upwards of 21,000, but divisions and disagreements amongst the high command had already begun, and were ultimately to prove fatal.

The Scots straggled south over fifty miles of what is now the A6, with the cavalry in front and the Ulster veterans in the rear. Meanwhile, the Royalists under Langdale marched to the east of the main body, through Yorkshire.

Cromwell, having been alerted to the Scots march while crushing a Royalist rebellion in Pembrokeshire, hurried north via Leicester and Nottingham and joined forces with Lambert near Knaresborough on August 13th. The combined strength of the two forces was scarcely 9,000 men, but this was the New Model Army, and this was Cromwell.

Leaving his artillery train behind to allow greater speed, Cromwell marched west and by 16th August had reached the Ribble bridge at Clitheroe. At a council of war the choice was debated whether to proceed south of the Ribble to block the Scots advance south of Preston, or to advance along the north bank of the river to try and take them in the flank, in or north of the town.

This bold plan was decided upon, and was perhaps Cromwell's only chance. A position south of Preston would have allowed Hamilton to wait in the comparative security of Preston for his whole army to assemble, and for the English Royalists to join them from the east. He could then have given battle on his own terms and probably overwhelmed Cromwell by sheer weight of numbers.

He was to be allowed neither the luxury of choosing the battleground nor the time to bring his forces together. Cromwell stayed the night of August 16th at Stonyhurst Hall and marched very early the next morning towards Preston, approaching the town along what is now Longridge Road.

He sent forward an advanced guard of two hundred horse and four hundred foot, who came upon a party of Langdale's Royalists on Ribbleton Moor and compelled them to retreat to their main body after a sharp engagement. Langdale's main force was well positioned astride of the route to Preston, probably just to the north-west of the present Blackpool Road/ Ribbleton Avenue junction.

At that time Ribbleton Lane was, in Cromwell's words, 'A lane very deep and ill,' and, once his whole army had assembled, Cromwell resolved to force this lane with cavalry and subsidiary attacks down each side of the road on a wide front to prevent flanking movements. Harrison's and Cromwell's own regiments were assigned to the central role, and the battle commenced. Langdale's force totalled around 4,000 and was heavily outnumbered, but put up stubborn resistance.

Back in Preston, the Scots cavalry had already arrived, crossed the Ribble bridge and were on their way to Wigan. As Cromwell launched his attack, the main body of the infantry were crossing the river with the rearguard still several miles north of the town. When messengers arrived with news of Langdale's plight, Hamilton issued an order for the cavalry to return, but his second-in-command, Callendar, urged that the infantry should not be allowed to give battle without cavalry support, and therefore that they should cross the Ribble, await the cavalry, and hold the river bridge until Langdale could fall back and join them. This plan not only included the needless sacrifice of Langdale's force, but also made ultimate defeat virtually certain. Hamilton was stupid enough to allow himself to be overruled and, apart from a small body of horse, he sent no help to Langdale.

After a heroic resistance for four hours, Langdale's force broke and fled down what are now Deepdale Road and Ribbleton Lane, into London Road and thence via Frenchwood to the old Ribble bridge, some 90 yards downstream from the present one. Others fled into the town, from which they were dislodged by Harrison's and Cromwell's regiments of horse and chased in the direction of Lancaster.

At the bridge most of the Scots had crossed and the bridge had been barricaded. Cromwell's troops fell upon the Royalists and Scots and a ferocious engagement ensued, often 'at push of pike', until the Ribble bridge was taken and, soon afterwards, the bridge over the Darwen. Night was falling by this time, and darkness and exhaustion combined to

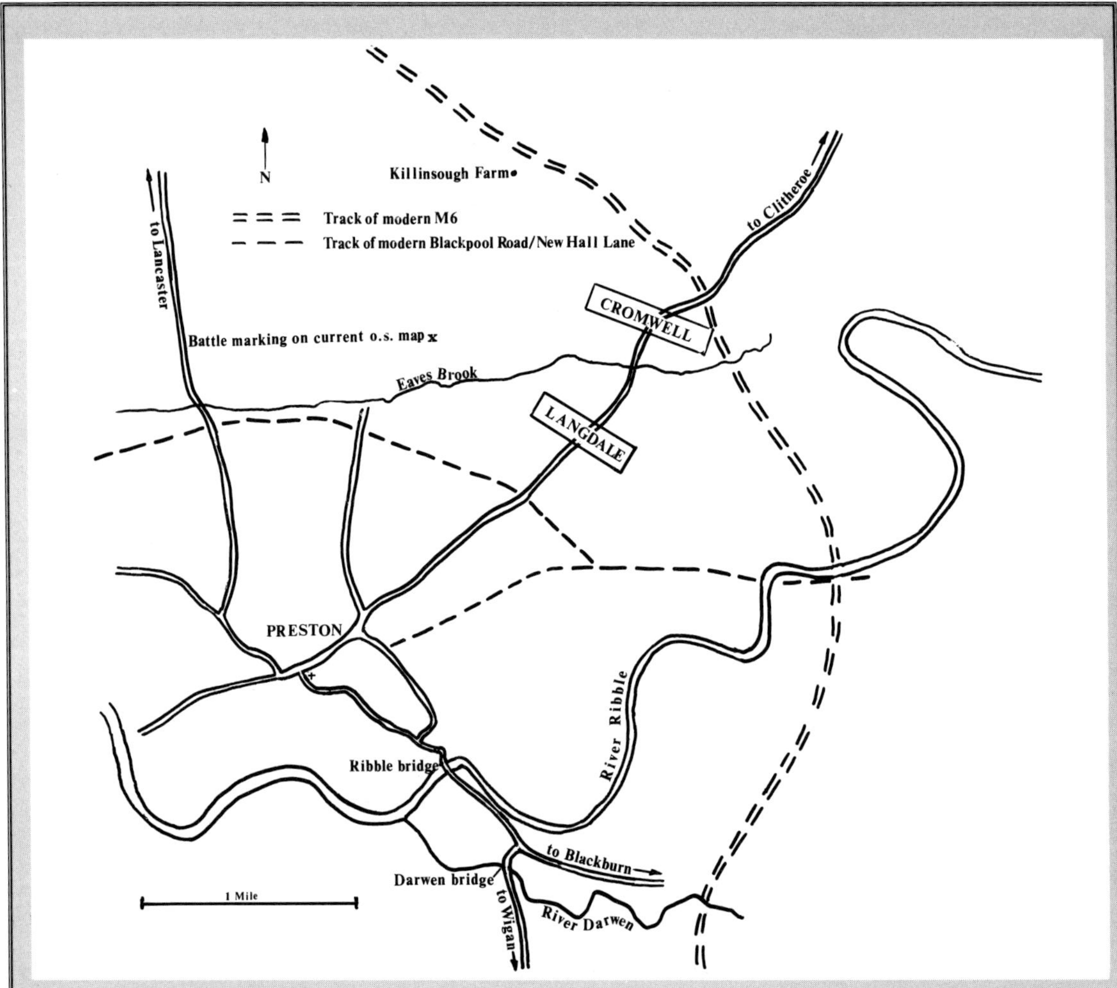

halt Cromwell's advance.

To the north, English Royalists and Scots had been chased ten miles towards Lancaster, with five hundred horses and many prisoners taken. In his despatch to Parliament, Cromwell estimated that the enemy had lost around 1,000 men killed with 4,000 prisoners, and many that escaped did so without their arms. Further to the north, the Ulster veterans, who had taken no part in the battle, were urged by English Royalists to advance to Preston to attack Cromwell. Monroe would have none of this, however, and retreated instead towards Scotland.

On the following day, August 18th, the pursuit southwards resumed, with 3,000 foot and 2,500 horse from Cromwell's army chasing the Scots, who still numbered more than 10,000. They were harried to Wigan and from there towards Warrington where they were forced to make a stand near Winwick. After sustaining 1,000 casualties and 2,000 prisoners, the foot surrendered, leaving the horse to be driven through Cheshire before surrendering at Uttoxeter on August 22nd. The remaining Lancashire Royalists were hunted through the North West before finally surrendering at Appleby on October 9th. Only then could the campaign which culminated in the Battle of Preston be said to have ended.

The Battle of Preston

Words: Gregg Butler, 1976
Music: ibid.

Praise to the Lord for this glorious victory,
Praise to the men by whose arms
This insurrection is sharply brought down.
Render praise and the singing of psalms.
Do not exult on the death of a foeman
But grieve for a soul that's set free.
Remember always it was for their God they died
Though 'twas the king paid their fee.

Darkness has now spread its web upon Preston,
Both living and dead are unseen.
Darkness is cloaking the Ribble at Preston
To hide the red cast in the stream.
Darkness hides weariness, pain and the horrors
That man can inflict upon men.
Darkness, a blessing, brings softness to evils,
Hides carnage and dulls the sharp pain.

Shall we be free from this warring and pestilence?
Is England now to be free?
Free to tend field, the pond and the orchard,
And free to cut fruit from the tree?
No more this warring of son against father,
Nor cousin by cousin be slain?
Let us pray this is so, but still hangs a dank feeling,
An omen of still pending pain.

Praise to the Lord for this glorious victory,
Praise to the men by whose arms
This insurrection is sharply brought down.
Render praise and the singing of psalms.

This, the only completely 'manufactured' song in the collection, was written for the production 'Vive le Roi' which was performed by Blackpool College Theatre Group in November 1976. Strawhead were commissioned to do the music, and everything was going fine until we found that the centrepiece of the show was to be 'a song about the Battle of Preston' and, having delved at length through the contemporary material, we knew there wasn't one! An Arts Council fee hung in the balance for several milliseconds before this song was persuaded to appear spontaneously on a sheet of lined A4! We hope the song tells its own story.

The King Enjoys His Own Again

Words: Condensed and slightly modified (Gregg Butler, 1991) from *The Loyal Subjects' exultation for the Coronation of King Charles the Second*, anon. (possibly F. Grove), 1660, EB158, 249.
Tune: Widespread from about 1640, for example ERUB 10 p8.
Reprinted PMOT 437.

What writers could prognosticate
Concerning England's happy fate?
Lilly, I think, could little see
The joyous state now come to be.
His almanacks told that Charles never should
Return o'er England's land to reign
But Lilly's a liar like the devil his sire
Now the king enjoys his own again.

Now what's become of Lambert's power?
Alas, he's prisoner in the Tower
And better days will now ensue
That ever yet poor England knew.
Then well may we sing for the joy of our king
A toast in sack we'll freely drain
For Charles is returned and the old rump is
   burned
Now the king enjoys his own again.

England was but a senseless trunk
Until she was restored by Monk.
Before his wrath the Rump has fled
As he's returned to us our head.
Oh, long let him stand to rule and command
Throughout the world renown attain
Let all England then say Amen and Amen
Now the king enjoys his own again.

Let every man with tongue and pen
Rejoice that Charles is come again
To gain his sceptre and his throne
And to give every man his own.
Let all tongues with joy loud cry 'Vive le Roy'
To freely now rejoice his fame
Let your sweet voices sing a 'God save the
   king'
Now the king enjoys his own again.

This song has been called 'the most famous and popular air'. It was probably written by Martin Parker round about 1642 and became the most popular Royalist song of the war. It was, not surprisingly, pressed into service after the interregnum and the present copy was issued for the coronation of Charles II. Parker's original had clearly stood up well to eighteen years of popularity and modification.

not survive him long, and Charles II was restored to the throne in 1660. In Preston, as elsewhere, the event was celebrated with a great show of loyalty and rejoicing.

None rejoiced more fervently or loyally than the mayor and corporation, so lately largely Parliamentarian in their sympathies – still, they got away with it, and received a new Charter in 1673.

This was withdrawn, however – no doubt when Charles discovered where their true sympathies lay. Undaunted, Preston procured the services of Judge Jeffreys – who was to become the 'hanging judge' of Monmouth's rebellion – to plead their case. He was wined, dined, flattered, and proved, in this instance at least, to be a man of his word – Preston got its new Charter in 1684.

When Charles died in 1685 the crown passed to his brother, James II. James was politically and governmentally inept; he was also overtly Catholic. He weathered the early Protestant challenge of Monmouth's rebellion but steadily lost the support of his nobles and parliament, and a bloodless coup in 1689 placed his daughter, Mary, on the throne with her Dutch Protestant husband, William of Orange.

However, support for the deposed king and his heirs remained strong in Preston and many other parts of the North West. These adherents to the old cause were now referred to as 'Jacobites'. In Preston there was a Jacobite 'mock' corporation at Walton-le-Dale. This was formed in 1701 and functioned openly as a Jacobite meeting society and club, contrasting greatly with the real corporation, which remained staunchly Presbyterian and supported the new monarchic line. In 1711 a certain Lord Derwentwater was 'Mayor'.

When Queen Anne died in 1714 the crown was passed to the Protestant George of Hanover. The Scots, already pro-Jacobite, were particularly incensed that the Stuart line had been ignored. When, on 6th September 1715, the Earl of Mar raised the Jacobite standard at Braemar, Derwentwater was one of the several English notables in the north to join the Scots in rebellion. They had convinced themselves (and the Scots) that Lancashire would rise to the cause, and so travelled the familiar route south, arriving at Preston on 10th November. They were hospitably entertained, but there was no sign of a general rising. The local High-Church Tories, who were much given to toasting James as 'King over the Water', said much but did nothing. No more than 200 recruits joined them from the town, all of them Catholic. Preston had clearly not yet identified a winning side!

The government had placed General Carpenter to cover the eastern route with the main army. On learning that the west side had again been used, he followed Cromwell's path over the Pennines as quickly as possible. Meanwhile, General Wills had assembled a force at Wigan and the road to the south was blocked.

The Jacobite leaders were lulled by their welcome, and were also frankly incompetent. They were in carnival mood – one wrote, 'The ladies in this town, Preston, are so very beautiful and richly attired that the gentlemen soldiers from Wednesday to Saturday minded nothing but courting and feasting'. No march, no entrenchment, no preparation to retreat.

Early on Saturday (12th November) Wills marched quickly from Wigan, arrived at Walton-le-Dale by 11 o'clock and captured the Ribble bridge which was unguarded – though in any case the tide was out, so the Ribble presented little obstacle. The rebels quickly barricaded Church Street at both ends, Tithebarn Street (then called Salter Lane), and the bottom of Fishergate and Friar-gate to seal the town.

At 2 o'clock Wills forced the first Church Street barrier, but his troops were then caught in a crossfire from the houses on either side and forced to retreat with heavy losses. Wills then mounted a house-to-house operation which eventually outflanked and destroyed the first Church Street barricade.

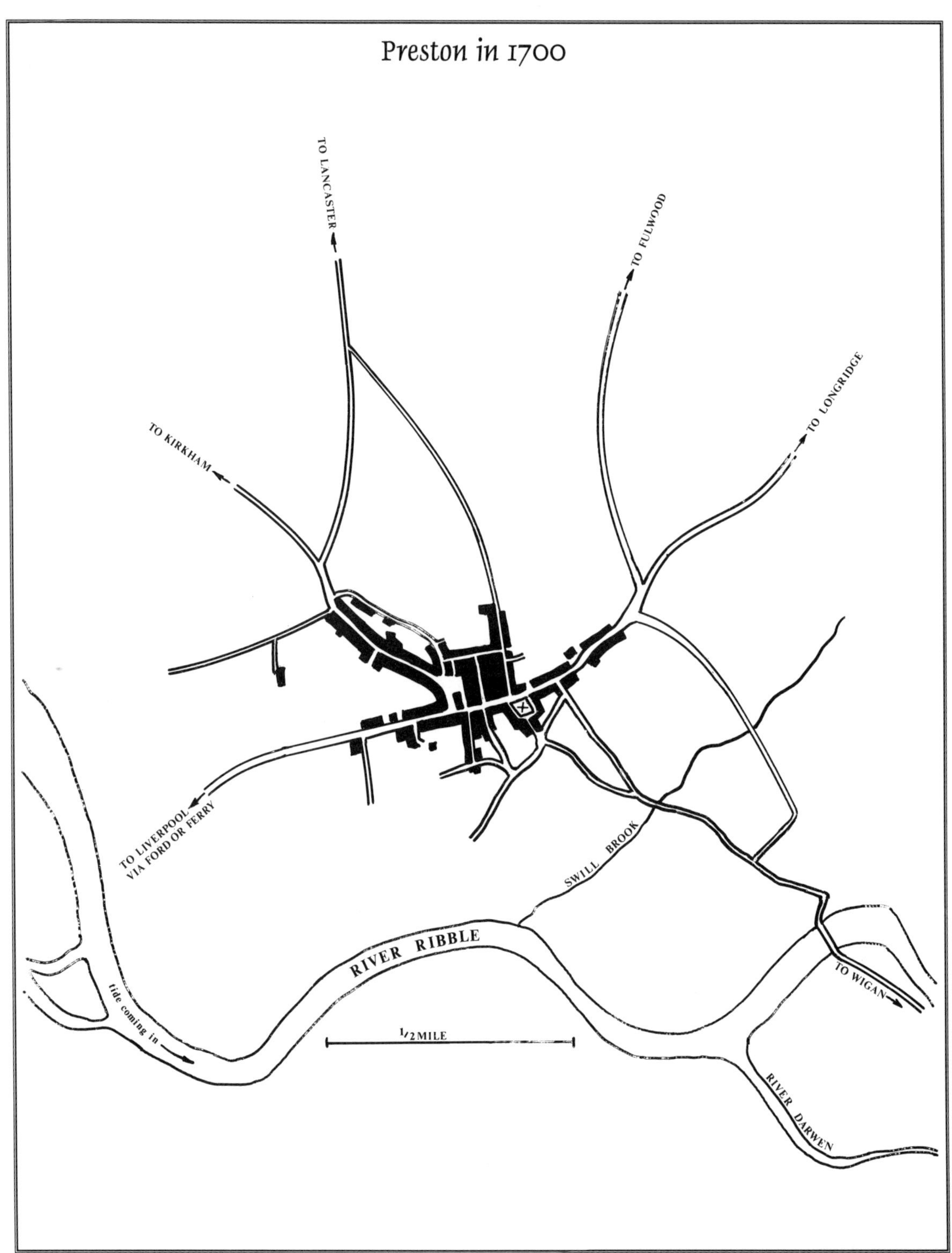

Preston in 1700
TO LANCASTER
TO FULWOOD
TO LONGRIDGE
TO KIRKHAM
TO LIVERPOOL VIA FORD OR FERRY
SWILL BROOK
RIVER RIBBLE
TO WIGAN
tide coming in
1/2 MILE
RIVER DARWEN

Meanwhile, a similar attack was taking place at the Friargate barricade. The Jacobites retained possession, but by the Saturday evening houses were burning at the ends of Friargate and Church Street, and the town was surrounded and sealed off.

On the Sunday morning, Carpenter arrived from Clitheroe with 2,500 men and generously put himself under Wills' command. The English Jacobites now tried to negotiate a private treaty with Wills without telling the Scots. Wills declared that he would only accept unconditional surrender. The Scots found out about this attempted parley and much confusion reigned in Preston for the rest of the Sunday, along with, one suspects, not a little acrimony. Meanwhile, Wills consolidated his position. At 7 o'clock on the Monday morning he was told of the rebels' unconditional surrender. The Jacobites handed over their weapons at the Mitre Inn, their headquarters in the market square. The town was then given over to the Royalist soldiers, 'who were allowed to plunder the houses of the innocent townspeople'.

The rank and file were imprisoned in the parish church. Of the officers, four were court-martialled immediately and shot against the church wall, and another twelve were hanged on Gallows Hill, just outside the town's northern boundary (later the site of English Martyrs' Church) following trial in Liverpool. A further 62 officers were transported. The leaders were taken to London and, though many were pardoned or escaped, Derwentwater was found guilty of high treason and beheaded on Tower Hill on 24th February 1716.

Continued on page 35

The Battle of Preston, 1715

The Jacobite army that marched south into Lancashire in 1715 was a mixture of Highland and Lowland Scots and English 'gentlemen volunteers' and their adherents.

The major Highland force was a detachment of the Earl of Mar's army – Clan Chattan – and other troops under the command of Brigadier MacIntosh. The Lowland Scots were headed by Lord Kenmure and the Earls of Nithsdale, Wintoun and Carnwath. The English contingent was relatively small and principally Catholic, consisting of the Earl of Derwentwater and Lord Widdrington with a few country gentlemen and their servants and tenants.

To have any hope of success the rebellion needed to spark off a major uprising in England against the Hanoverian establishment. It was for this reason that Lancashire was the chosen route, as the large number of local Catholics and pro-Jacobite, High Church Tories were said to be ripe for rebellion, and in fact Lord Widdrington assured the Scots that 20,000 men could be expected to flock to James III's colours in Lancashire. It was, however, obvious that a successful uprising could not be based on Catholic recruits alone, and neither was it likely that an uprising would be triggered by an army commanded by a Scot. It was therefore essential that the insurgents gave the command to someone who was both English and impeccably Protestant. The problem was that such persons were in distinctly short supply.

The only commander with any military stature was Brigadier MacIntosh, an old and experienced soldier; few of the English gentlemen had done much fighting, and all of these were Catholic. The command therefore devolved to Thomas Forster, a country squire without any knowledge or experience in the art of war. That he was both English and Protestant were his only qualifications for command, and the inadequacy of those qualifications was brutally laid bare in the ensuing campaign.

The Anglo-Scots force marched from the border via Penrith, Appleby and Kendal. Reaching Lancaster on 7th November 1715, they seized six guns from a ship at Sunderland Point and then set off via Garstang to Preston, which the horse entered on 9th November and the foot the following day.

Some recruits had been picked up on the march south, but only a few tens in number and virtually all of them Catholic. In fact, the recruitment of a Protestant, Mr. Muncaster of Garstang, was a matter of some considerable celebration. By the time they entered Preston, some writers put the number of the Anglo-Scots force at over 4,000, but the actual numbers are unlikely to have exceeded half this figure.

The foot marched straight to the market cross, 'where they were drawn up . . . while the Pretender was proclaimed. Here they were also joined by a great many gentlemen, with their tenants, servants and attendants, and some of very good figure in the country, but still all papists'.[1] In fact, the recruits numbered around two hundred – by far the largest number to join on the march, but still far short of the 20,000 which Lord Widdrington had led Forster to expect.

Preston gave the Jacobites a notable welcome and Peter Clarke, an attorney's clerk who had joined the expedition at Kendal, noted that 'The ladies in this town Preston are so very beautiful and so richly attired that the gentlemen soldiers from Wednesday to Saturday minded nothing but courting and feasting'.[2]

This inactivity (or rather, lack of military activity!) was against the background that the very same Lancashire gentleman who had assured Forster that 20,000 recruits would be forthcoming, now assured him that no Government troops could come within forty miles of Preston without being infallibly reported. In fact, it seems certain that Forster knew on 9th November of Government forces at Wigan, but elected to do nothing.

On the Government side, the generals in the field were Carpenter and Wills, but behind them was a Hanoverian military machine honed by the wars of the Spanish succession and directed by that master strategist, the Duke of Marlborough. This particular playing field was never even remotely level.

General Carpenter had assumed that the rebels would strike east from Carlisle to Newcastle and, realising his mistake, he marched south-west via Durham and Barnard Castle towards Preston. Meanwhile, Wills had gathered together various regiments from Chester, Manchester and as far afield as Worcester, and mustered them at Wigan.

On Friday 11th November Derwentwater received news that Wills would march on Preston and attack on the 12th. Forster was told the news, appeared dispirited, and went to bed. Somewhat alarmed, the other leaders held a council and ordered the detachment of an advanced guard towards Wigan, the securing of the Darwen and Ribble bridges, and the readying of the whole army for battle. At this juncture Forster awoke and countermanded these orders – apathy prevailed!

By the Sunday morning Forster seemed to have disregarded the report of Wills' advance, and actually gave orders for the whole army to march from Preston towards Manchester. This order was immediately reversed when, soon after daylight, the vanguard of Wills' army was seen approaching from the direction of Walton-le-Dale. Initially a force was sent to secure the bridge, but was later withdrawn into the town on the advice of Brigadier MacIntosh, who pronounced the bridge undefendable because the river was so easily forded, it being low tide.

MacIntosh was aware that his Highland infantry would have little chance in a set-piece battle against cavalry, and counselled that the only chance was to stay within the town, using buildings and enclosed spaces to reduce the effectiveness of cavalry attack. This tactic was, however, essentially defensive and offered no hope of eventual victory against the Hanoverian war machine. It is quite likely that MacIntosh (though not Forster) knew this, but chose at least to postpone the inevitable.

Wills arrived at midday and was amazed to find the bridge unguarded and, having placed forces above the Ribble bridge and the Penwortham ford, he planned to attack simultaneously up Wigan Lane/ Churchgate from the east, and down Friargate from the north-west.

Meanwhile, the insurgents had finally woken up to their danger and were frenziedly active in entrenching themselves and throwing up barricades. One barrier blocked Churchgate below the

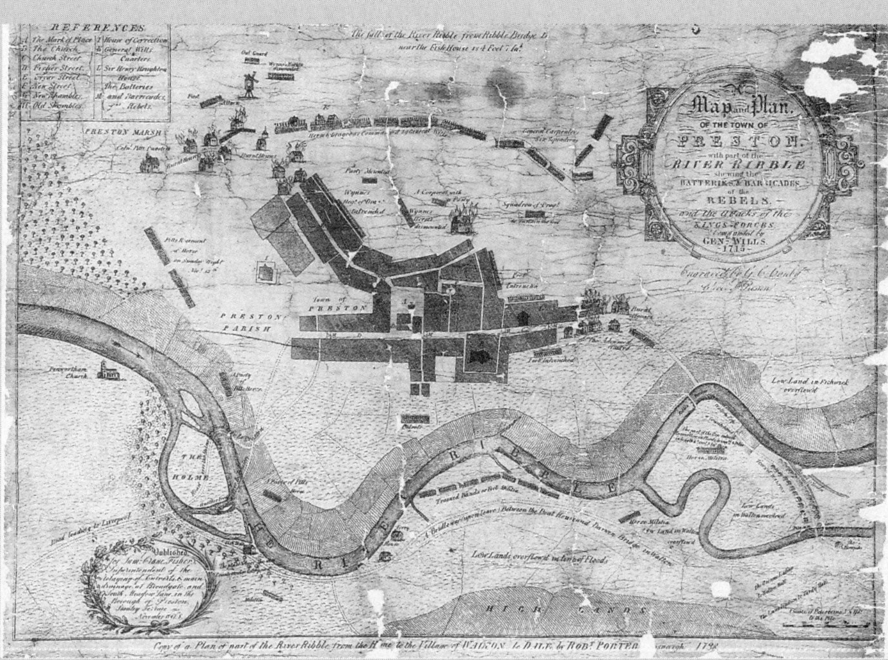

eastern end of the churchyard, a second blocked the lane running into Churchgate from the north, a third was on Friargate and a fourth on Fishergate. Various troops were placed in the houses lining these entrances to the town and the main reserve was marshalled in the market square. Around two o'clock in the afternoon, two hundred of Wills' men attacked the Churchgate barrier. They were met by a withering fire from the barrier itself and from the houses on either side. A cannon was also positioned in the churchyard and although the first shot removed a nearby chimney (the seaman-gunner being a trifle drunk), the next shots did considerable damage and contributed to the failure of the attack with the loss of some one hundred men.

The Government troops then managed to fire the houses and barns at the entrance to Churchgate and the Highlanders who had been firing from them were forced further into the town. Churchgate was next commanded by the large, battlemented mansion of Sir Henry Houghton and the house of Mr. Ayres opposite. These houses had been strongly garrisoned by the Jacobites, but for some reason Forster had ordered the troops off on another errand and the houses were promptly taken, though not without loss, by the Government. Forster would not allow an attack to retake the houses, and this left the Churchgate position fatally weakened. Meanwhile, the barrier guarding the lane to the north, whose defence was led by Lord Charles Murray, was heavily attacked but, with the aid of reinforcements rushed over from the churchyard, the attack was repulsed with considerable losses.

The barricade in Friargate was attacked at four o'clock in the afternoon. Here, too, the Highlanders defended bravely and repulsed the attack with heavy losses. Once more the Government troops fired the houses as near to the barricade as they could reach. With night now approaching both armies tried to rest, and Forster, as somnolent by day as by night, went to bed.

It had been discovered that Wills had neglected to block the west end of Fishergate with troops, and many of the Jacobites slunk off under cover of darkness and made their way north. For reasons only known to himself, Wills ordered that the windows of all the houses held by the Government be illuminated. This was duly done and illuminated the streets, making passing Jacobites easy targets. It also silhouetted the people who were doing the firing and made them vulnerable. Another command to extinguish the lights was misunderstood, with the result that ever more candles were lit, but by now both sides were well hidden and the lights shone on empty streets and windows!

There were minor house-to-house actions throughout the night, and more houses and barns were burned, but certainly as Sunday dawned the Jacobites had so far repulsed all that Wills could throw at them, and had inflicted quite heavy casualties while taking very few of their own.

At ten o'clock on Sunday 13th November, however, General Carpenter arrived at the end of his march from Newcastle with 2,500 horse and dragoons. The fate of the army in the town was sealed.

Initially Carpenter, though the senior officer, deferred to Wills in the light of the latter's glowing reports of the affairs to date. After surveying the town, however, Carpenter seems to have realised that all was not well, and in particular moved quickly to close off the end of Fishergate and complete the encirclement of the town. The few that still tried to escape were cut down.

Finding that they were completely surrounded, the Highlanders now wished to sally out and attack, but Forster, persuaded by Lord Widdrington and a few others (and unknown to the bulk of the army) immediately decided to sue for terms and, around two o'clock, sent a Colonel Oxborough to General Wills. Wills refused surrender as prisoners of war, but gave Forster one hour to decide whether to surrender at discretion. This simply meant that they would not be cut down there and then but would be subject to any punishment that the Government might order. If these terms were not accepted then the Government troops would attack.

Meanwhile, the Scots, noting the absence of activity on the Government side, began to suspect that negotiations were going on to which they were not a party. Initial demands for an immediate sally were reconsidered, and in the event the Scots sent out their own emissary, Captain Dalziel, to negotiate with Wills. This they did before the hour given by Wills to Colonel Oxborough had expired, and on being offered the same terms the Scots asked for more time to decide – until 7 o'clock the next day.

By now there was an irreconcilable breach within the town between the English, who wanted to surrender, and the Highland troops, who still favoured a fight. There were various scuffles between the two factions and at least one man was killed. After much to-ing and fro-ing, Wills allowed them the time they had asked for, on condition that no fresh barricades were erected and no-one tried to leave the town.

No sooner had this been agreed when six or seven of the English Jacobites attempted to ride out of the town but were intercepted and cut to pieces. Carpenter then insisted on a Scots and an English hostage for the Jacobites' good behaviour, and eventually the Earl of Derwentwater and Colonel MacIntosh surrendered themselves.

At seven o'clock on the Monday morning the armistice expired. Much of the army still did not know what terms had been agreed, and when they found out they were all for fighting their way out to the north. They were with difficulty persuaded to surrender. The noblemen were allowed to surrender in private in the Mitre Tavern, and the other officers and men laid down their arms in the churchyard and were confined in the church.

Six of the officer prisoners were tried for desertion by courts martial at Preston, and four of them were shot. The chief prisoners were taken to London, where Derwentwater and Lord Kenmure were found guilty of high treason and beheaded. Forster, the Earl of Nithsdale, Brigadier MacIntosh and Derwentwater's brother, Charles Radcliffe, managed to escape to the continent – though Radcliffe was captured thirty years later and executed on the 1715 charge.

Seventy-four further prisoners were tried the following January and twelve were executed in Preston on Gallows Hill, now the site of English Martyrs Church.

Thomas Forster, surely the most undeserving soul of this or any other rebellion, escaped to the continent and lived there for many years, dying of 'an asthma' in Boulogne on 3rd November 1738.

1. Peter Patten, reported in Lancashire Memorials 1715, Chetham Soc., V (1848), 100.
2. Peter Clarke, ibid, 107.

Derwentwater

James Radcliffe, 3rd Earl of Derwentwater, was born in London on 28th June 1689. He was the eldest son of Edward, the 2nd Earl, by Lady Mary Tudor, a daughter of Charles II by Mary Davis, a noted actress of the time. As was quite usual for Charles' many bastard children, Mary was granted the precedence of a duke's daughter and consequently married well.

The title had been conferred on the family by James II in 1688, and the young James Radcliffe followed the king into exile in 1689, being brought up as a companion to the young prince James Edward, until the death of the second Earl in 1705. Derwentwater travelled extensively on the continent and did not sail for England until 1709, visiting his Cumberland estates for the first time in 1710. His arrival in the area was clearly a boost to Jacobite hopes, and it is significant that he was made 'Mayor' of the Jacobite corporation of Walton-le-Dale as early as 1711.

A devoted Jacobite and a Roman Catholic, as well as a Stuart by lineage, he joined the 1715 Jacobite conspiracy and subsequent rebellion almost without thought. He had, of course, been suspected of disloyal sentiments by the Hanoverian government, and on the eve of the insurrection a warrant was signed for his arrest. The news reached Derwentwater well before the warrant, and he went into hiding until the Scots raised the standard of the Pretender. He then raised a company of gentlemen and armed servants from his estate and rode to join the rising at Greenrig on 6th October 1715.

After the march south, Derwentwater was taken prisoner at the Battle of Preston. He was examined before the Privy Council on 10th January 1716 and impeached with the other lords on 19th January. He pleaded guilty, urging as extenuating circumstances his inexperience and his role in minimising loss of life at Preston.

He was found guilty and condemned to death.

Great efforts were made to have him pardoned, with petitions to the Houses of Parliament and an address to the throne. Various other notable prisoners were reprieved but the King was determined to make an example of Derwentwater, and obdurately refused a pardon.

Derwentwater was beheaded on Tower Hill on 24th February 1716, expressing on the scaffold his regret at having pleaded guilty, his devotion to the Roman Catholic religion and to James III. Derwentwater's body was buried at St. Giles-in-the-Fields but was subsequently taken to Dilston and there interred in the Derwentwater vault until 1874, when it was again moved to where it now rests at Thornden in Essex.

The death of Derwentwater excited considerable sympathy. He was a young man of noble bearing and simple motives, and in his brief time in the North of England he had become extremely popular. It was inevitable that songs would be sung about his death, but quite exceptional that these should have become so widespread, and persisted long enough to be collected from singers in the nineteenth and twentieth centuries in places as far afield as Hampshire, Scotland, Georgia and Florida.

Lord Derwentwater

Words: Traditional, collated from five versions in TTCB 3 264–267.
Tune: ibid, tune 2, p265, from the singing of 'Happy' Flack at Foulmire, July
121907, via the Vaughan Williams MSS 1, 89.

Our king has written a long letter
And sealed it over with gold
And sent it to Lord Derwentwater
To read it if he could.

He has not sent it with a boy
He sent it by no page
But sent it by as gallant a knight
As e'er did combat wage.

The first lines Derwentwater read
They caused him great surprise
But the next lines that he did read
Made the tears start from his eyes.

'Oh saddle to me my milk white steed
'Prepare it with all speed,
'For I must away to fair London Town
'For of me there was ne'er more need.'

He had not rode a mile but one
When his horse stumbled on a stone,
''Tis a token,' said Lord Derwentwater,
'That I shall ne'er more return.'

And when they came to fair London Town
And into the Courtiers' hall
The Lords and Knights of fair London Town
Did him a traitor call.

'A traitor, a traitor,' says my lord,
'A traitor, how can that be?
'For I have kept five thousand fighting men
'To fight for King Jamie.'

Then up there stepped a grey old man,
With a sword drawn in his hand,
'There stands the block Lord Derwentwater,
'Your life is at my command'.

'But give me leave,' Derwentwater said,
'To speak words two or three
'Ye Lord and Ladies of London town
'Be kind to my lady.'

'There's fifty pounds in my right pocket,
'Divide it to the poor,
'And fifty in my left pocket,
'Divide it from door to door.

He laid his head upon the block
The sword was sharp and strong
The stroke that cut his suffering short
Preserved his memory long.

A thoroughly traditional ballad collected by Vaughan Williams in 1907 and with a traditional history traceable to the mid-18th century. The five versions quoted in TTCB range from an 1827 version collected in Paisley via the 1907 version used to one collected in 1937 in Florida. Clearly Derwentwater's fate struck a popular chord, and this Prestonian event is probably the most recent to enter the mainstream of traditional balladry.

The death of this seemingly obscure if dashing nobleman caught public fancy and was commemorated in a song which then travelled widely, changing and developing as it went. It endured, and many variants were still being sung throughout the British Isles and North America even in this century. Thus did one small chapter of Preston's history achieve a curious immortality.

In 1724 Daniel Defoe, author of *Robinson Crusoe*, toured Britain and published a book describing the various places he had visited — an early version of the modern guide-books. His description of Preston clearly shows a town still in a state of shock even after nine years.

The flames of rebellion were fanned again in 1745. James' son, Charles Edward Stuart, sailed from France to Scotland, raised the Scots clans at Glenfinane, and won a victory over the government troops near Edinburgh. From then on history repeated itself as Bonny Prince Charlie (as he was known) marched south through Carlisle and Lancaster to Preston, which he reached on November 27th. Once more the hoped-for flood of recruits did not arrive and he marched on, to the sound of the Preston Town Band playing *When the King enjoys his Own again* to speed him on his way. By 12th December he was back, marching urgently in the opposite direction to his fate at Culloden, pursued closely by Oglethorpe's Dragoons, and was sped on his way once more by Preston Town Band — this time playing the anti-Jacobite hit of the day, *Hie Thee Charlie Home Again*.

One young woman who did seem anxious to see the would-be king was Peggy from Long

Extract from Daniel Defoe's

Tour through the whole Island of Great Britain (1724)

Preston is a fine town, and tolerably full of people, but not like Liverpool or Manchester; besides, we come now beyond the trading part of the county. Here's no manufacture; the town is full of attorneys, proctors and notaries, the process of law being of a different nature than it is in other places, it being a dutchy and a county palatine, and having particular priveleges of its own. The people are gay here, though not perhaps the richer for that; but it has by that obtained the name of Proud Preston. Here is a good deal of good company, but not so much, they say, as was before the late bloody action with the northern rebels; not that the battle hurt many of the immediate inhabitants, but so many families there and thereabout have been touched by the consequences of it, that it will not be recovered in a few years, and they seem to have a kind of remembrance of things upon them still.

(Defoe's spelling and punctuation.)

Preston near Settle. She hiked the 38 miles to Preston, saw Prince Charlie and returned to Ribblesdale to tell of it. The song which recorded the incident has survived in the area only in fragments, but at one time it must have been widely known, and a version printed in London has provided the rest of the story. Suffice to say that she was not merely a spectator.

Long Preston Peggy

Words: Verse 1 traditional, printed BSL 83, remainder from *Long Waisted Peggy*, a
broadside ballad from the Madden Collection, reprinted LEBB 2 11 p39.
Tune: *Chevy Chase*, traditional, as printed TTCB 3 116, tune 8 – but in 6/8 rather than 3/4.

Long Preston Peggy to Proud Preston went,
To view the Scotch rebels it was her intent
And as she was singing a Scotch lord came by
And on pretty Peggy he fixed his eye.
He called to his servants who on him did wait,
'Go fetch me that fair maid that sings at my gate.
She sings so delightful, her voice is so clear
She's better to me than five thousand,
She's better to me than five thousand a year'.

'Here's fifty bright guineas I'll give unto thee
To buy you rich clothing and wearing to be
If that you are willing and want to comply
One night in my chamber with me for to lie.'
She took the Scotch lord by the lily-white hand,
She jumped into bed and the bargain did stand
When the tune of his oboe began for to play
O'er hill and down dales and so far,
O'er hills and down dales and so far away.

She liked well his music but it lulled him to sleep.
Then out of his chamber pretty Peggy did creep
With his rings and his jewels so costly and gay,
She left the Scotch lord on his oboe to play
O'er the hills and down dales and so far away.

Now Long Preston Peg's back in merry Yorkshire
She vows and declares she's a loose girl no more,
Unless it's a soldier who's deeply in want
That the girls of old England may never,
That the girls of old England may never grow scant.

This song tells the story of an encounter between a lass from Long Preston and Prince Charles Edward's army as they passed through Preston during the 1745 Jacobite rebellion. Only the first verse was collected traditionally in the mid-nineteenth century and many Lancashire antiquaries had a field day trying to 'reconstruct' the ballad. A Mr. Holroyd came up with 24 4-line stanzas which have Peggy joining the Pretender's army (with a total absence of amorous activity) and leading the taking of Manchester with only 'a sergeant and a drummer'.

What the song was really like was only discovered when research for this volume turned up a ninteenth-century broadside version printed and sold in London by J. Pitts. This had an identical first verse to the traditional Preston version, apart from Peggy coming from Bristol, and the rest of the song fitted so well into the traditional mould that here, undoubtedly, is the original set of words.

The tune is referred to as *Chevy Chase* in many sources, but at first glance the words do not fit well to any of the traditional versions of that tune. This problem was solved by the discovery that one of the 3/4 tunes fits the words well (if strenuously) when changed to 6/8 time.

And so, after a gap of well over 150 years, Long Preston Peggy rides again!

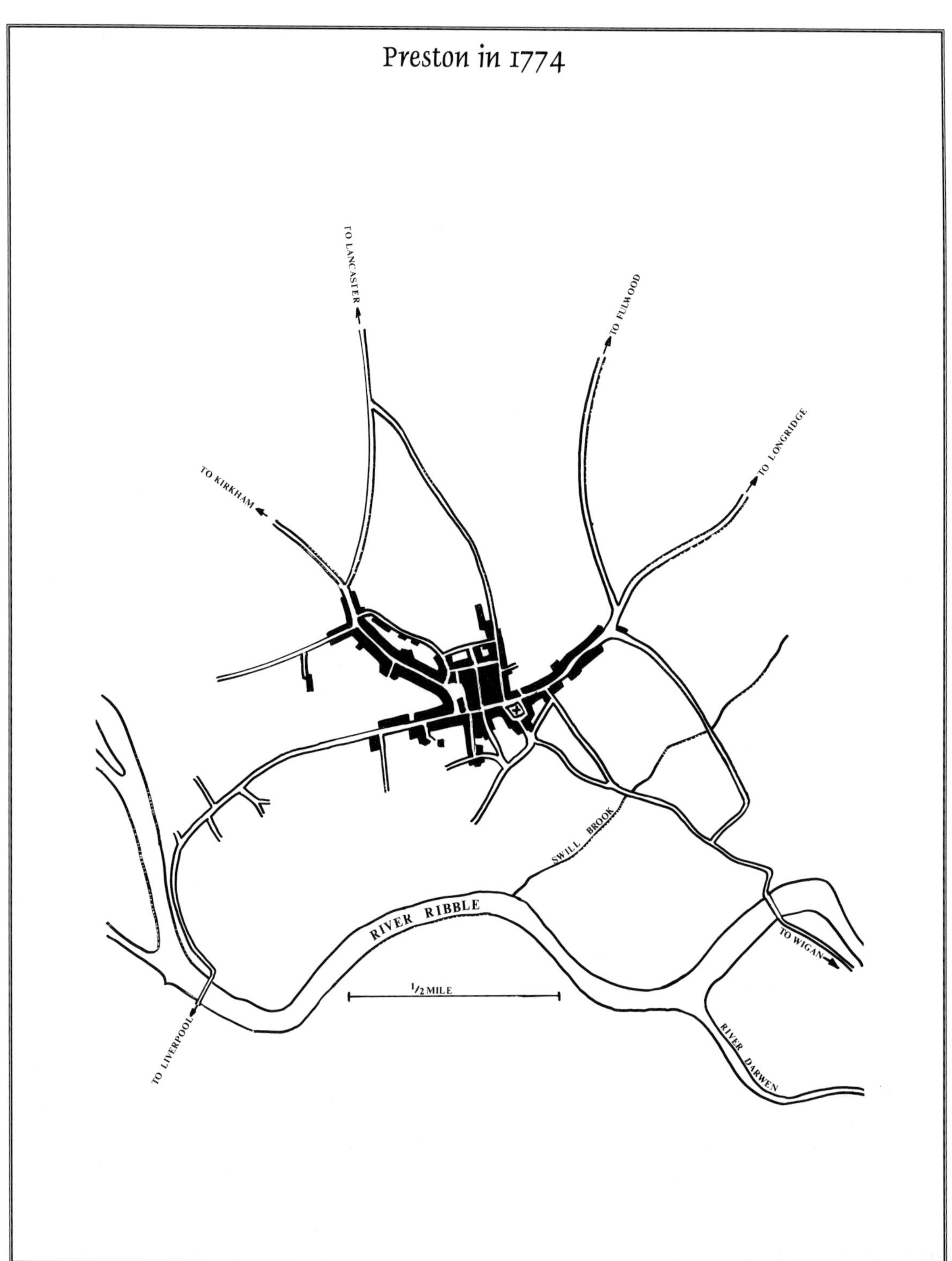

Preston in 1774
TO LANCASTER
TO FULWOOD
TO LONGRIDGE
TO KIRKHAM
TO WIGAN
SWILL BROOK
RIVER RIBBLE
1/2 MILE
TO LIVERPOOL
RIVER DARWEN

PART III

'The Cotton Lords of Preston . . .'

BY the Guild of 1762 the physical scars of the violence of the preceding hundred years had disappeared from the town and its surroundings as the people concentrated on their livelihoods with their customary pragmatism. However, if, after its previous rude awakening, the town thought that it could snuggle once more under its cosy eiderdown of obscurity, it was due for a nasty shock. Fate had dictated that it was to continue to provide the cockpit for equally bitter struggles.

The Age of Enlightenment had dawned across Europe. Men of intellect were beginning to challenge all the old orders and balances that had hitherto been undisputed.

In the countryside, England led the way in experimenting with new scientific methods of improving crops and stock to help feed a growing population. Those farmers that prospered were able to extend their operations. This speeded the process of enclosure of land with hedges and walls to aid their methods, which in turn created the familiar patchwork landscape to replace the open commons, heath and cultivation strips.

It also meant that less successful or less powerful tenants were squeezed out, forcing them to form a new under-class of hired agricultural labourers in place of the previous semi-co-operative rural communities of earlier years. Others sought work in towns, or were supported in poverty by the parish. Subsequent generations saw this process snowball as larger farmers became greedy for land and more niggardly with their rates of pay.

Other men experimented with new methods of manufacture, especially where machines could duplicate repetitive processes without requiring sleep, meal-breaks or payment. In the north-west such men looked especially at the processes of the thriving local cottage industry of spinning and weaving. This had long been a staple of full- and part-time self-employment in town and country; Lancashire favoured cotton textiles because its damp climate helped prevent the delicate threads from breaking. Needless to say, such mechanisation was unpopular since it threatened livelihoods in a secure but labour-intensive industry. Preston, which around the 1770s boasted about 6,000 inhabitants, formed the north-western corner of the cotton country that extended east and south through the Lancashire uplands.

Thus, when Blackburn's James Hargreaves invented a simple machine to perform part of

Continued on page 42

When This Old Hat Was New

Words: 'Noted in Leicestershire' SOH.
Tune: ibid.

I'm a poor old man in years, come listen to my song
Provisions now are twice as dear as when that I was
    young
When this old hat was new and stood upon my brow
Oh what a happy youth was I when this old hat was
    new.

It is but four score years ago, the truth I will declare
When men they took each other's words they thought it
    very fair
No oaths or bonds they did require, men's words they
    were so true
This was in my youthful days when this old hat was
    new.

When the time of harvest came and men went out to
    shear
How often we were merry made with brandy, wine and
    beer
And when the corn it was brought home and put upon
    the mow
Labourers' paunches were well-filled when this old hat
    was new.

The farmer at the board head stood the table for to grace
And greeted all as they came in and took their proper
    place
The wife she at the table stood to give each man his due
And oh what plenty did abound when this old hat was
    new.

But now the times are altered, the poor are quite done
    o'er
They give to them their wages like beggars at the door
Into the house we must no go although we are but few
It was not so when Bess did reign when this old hat
    was new.

The commons they are taken in and the cottages pulled
    down
Moll has got no wool to sew her linsey-woolsey gown
The weather's cold and clothing thin and blankets are
    but few
But we were clothed both back and skin when this old
    hat was new.

When Romans in this land did reign the commons they did give
Unto the poor in charity to help them for to live
But now the poor are quite done o'er we know it to be true
It was not so when Bess did reign and this old hat was new.

The song is based on an original theme of nostalgia for times past (from Martin Parker *circa* 1650 according to SOH. It was updated at the end of the eighteenth century to reflect the changes caused by Enclosure. We tried to use its original tune, *Old Sir Simon the King*, but it did not sit easily with the newer words so we retained the later melody.

Richard Arkwright

Of all the Prestonians who over the years have attained great fame or notoriety, Richard Arkwright must be counted the most remarkable. Yet so accustomed are we to the changes that he wrought within society that we now can scarcely recognise how fundamental they were in their day. Nor can we fail to be impressed by the man himself, no matter what view we take of his legacy.

Firstly, born in 1732 in a house in Lord Street, he started life from no privileged background, but, given a limited schooling, he continued to educate himself for the rest of his life. His remarkable mind applied itself to the problem of mechanisation of the spinning process, which had not changed since biblical times, and conceived a revolutionary process for the drawing and twisting of thread, not by emulating the human movements (as did the 'Spinning Jenny'), but using a system of spindles rotating at different speeds to produce a strong, even thread. Many would have stopped here, satisfied with that achievement, but he continued adapting and refining his 'frame' until in a continuous serial process the machine could perform all the tasks required to turn raw cotton into high- quality thread (1775). The machine process has required minimal additional development to this day.

Secondly (and this was perhaps his more important legacy), he devised the equally revolutionary idea of the factory. Although these existed already, in some senses of the word, it was Arkwright who visualised the concept of the factory worker trained to assist the machine, rather than the machine to assist the worker. At Cromford in Derbyshire he built in 1771 a six- storey 'factory' to accommodate his latest design of frames, powered by a great waterwheel turned by a stream from a warm spring (so as not to freeze in winter). The factory workers were housed in accommodation hard by, and their work periods were signalled by the peals of a great brass bell. In place of the time-honoured customs and frequently inefficient practices of the artisans' shops of other trades, Arkwright introduced the disciplines of work to match the speed of the machine, together with rules on cleanliness and safety. Arkwright seems to have treated his workers well, if strictly, and his advice was sought frequently by the 'model factory' builders. His son also carried on the tradition of looking after the welfare of his workers; the 'Satanic' character of mills came with a later generation of masters.

Thirdly, he turned to engineering and manufacture as a second career at the age of 34. Up to then he had built up a successful business as a barber and wig-maker in Bolton, particularly on the strength of a secret process for permanently dyeing hair. When the wig industry collapsed along with the fashion, it was the spur he needed to return to his native Preston (1767), obtain some financial backing, and commence development of his machine. Such was his belief in his machines and his planned use of them that he continued to battle on through all manner of obstacles and disappointments without ever losing confidence in his destiny. For most of his remaining years he worked from five in the morning till nine at night, in spite of troublesome asthma. He responded to local prejudice by moving to Derbyshire and finding new backers (1769). In the face of the refusal of Lancashire weavers to use his new yarn, he set up his own weaving mills and produced the finest stockings and calico that had been seen in the country (1773). Later he fought a series of lawsuits to protect his patents (1780–83); although he was unsuccessful in the courts he was never discouraged, and in any case as a manufacturer he was always ahead of the competition. He admitted that his greatest blow had been the destruction of his latest and finest mill in Chorley by masked rioters in 1779. Ever innovative, his Nottingham mill was the first mill to be powered by a steam engine (1790), one designed by James Watt.

He made a vast personal fortune: he was always convinced he would. All of it was re-invested in the business except in the last few years of his life, when he diverted some of it to his own comfort at last, and also to the improvement of the town of Cromford. Recognition came also in the form of a knighthood from George III in 1786. He died in 1792 aged 59.

The Water Frame

Copied from the original drawings attached to the specifications in the Patent Office.

'Now know ye that I, the said Richard Arkwright, do hereby describe and ascertain the nature of my said invention, and declare that the plan thereof drawn in the margin of these presents is composed of the following particulars, (that is to say) A, the Cogg Wheel and Shaft, which receive their motion from a horse. B, the Drum or Wheel which turns C, a belt of leather, and gives motion to the whole machine. D, a lead weight, which keeps F, the small drum, steady to E, the forcing Wheel. G, the shaft of wood which gives motion to the Wheel H, and continues it to I, four pairs of Rollers, (the form of which are drawn in the margin,) which act by tooth and pinion made of brass and steel nuts fixt in two iron plates K. That part of the roller which the cotton runs through is covered with wood, the top Roller with leather, and the bottom one fluted, which lets the Cotton, &c. through it; by one pair of Rollers moving quicker than the other, draws it finer for twisting, which is performed by the spindles T. K, the two iron plates described above. L, four large Bobbins with cotton rovings on conducted between Rollers at the back. M, the four threads carried to the Bobbins and Spindles by four small wires fixt across the frame in the slip of wood V. N, iron leavers with small lead weights hanging to the Rollers by Pulleys, which keep the Rollers close to each other. O, a cross piece of wood to which the leavers are fixed. P, the Bobbins and Spindles, Q, Flyers made of wood, with small wires on the side, which lead the thread to the Bobbins. R, small worsted bands put about the whirl of the bobbins, the screwing of which tight or easy causes the bobbins to wind up the thread faster or slower. S, the four whirls of the spindles. T, the four Spindles, which run in iron plates. V, explained in letter M. W, a wooden frame of the whole machine.

---

the spinning process, he soon found his new 'factory' wrecked by rioters in 1768. In that same year a Preston barber called Richard Arkwright had invented a wooden machine powered by water which could perform the entire spinning process. This was the most significant step forward in textile manufacture since the invention of the spinning- wheel, but he prudently moved to Nottingham before setting up the first of the many spinning mills that made his fortune.

The 'water frame' paved the way for a host of improvements over the next thirty years. By 1790 metal machines powered hundreds of spindles simultaneously.

Preston had a number of these mills, but the most significant step was taken by an energetic Bolton man who had come to Preston to experiment with machinery. With local backers he set up a series of spinning mills, the largest of these being the great 'Yellow Mill' on the outskirts of the town in Stanley Street. This man's name was John Horrocks.

Nearby, in New Hall Lane Fields, Horrocks built handloom weaving sheds and accommodation to encourage weavers to ply their trade close by (the first industrial estate, known as 'New Preston'). With yarn available in such quantity, the handloom weavers were able to operate a three-day week, to the scandalisation of the rest of Preston – indulging their favourite pursuits of cock-fighting and ferreting on the 'holy days of Saints Monday, Tuesday and Wednesday', as some commentators sourly remarked. During this period the population doubled to 12,000. This was the golden age of the handloom weaver, but it was destined to last for no more than a couple of years.

The Age of Enlightenment also challenged the political status quo, and Preston echoed the seething political debates of the time. America and France both underwent violent revolution.

Northerners, with their reputation for sturdy independence and blunt speech already established, joined in all the arguments with gusto. Lancashire, in fact, stood out from the rest of the country in its egalitarian spirit. One commentator remarked, 'It is sometimes said that Lancashire politics are "America-and-water". We suspect that it is America and very little water'. Preston had its own Jacobin club, presumably in honour of the political party in France which had executed the king.

The English ruling classes looked in fear at the possibility of copycat toff-topping and introduced various measures to combat sedition. Unions, political societies and clubs were infiltrated by spies and agents, denounced and finally outlawed as William Pitt and the old order resisted the new mood of the times. Other powerful men set up patriotic organisations and, under the guise of the threat from France, a militia was set up in every town. Preston merited an entire regiment.

While the abundance of yarn from the mills had made the hand-spinner obsolete, people flocked into Lancashire to try their hand at handloom weaving (for the weaving mills were not yet generally active). Preston's population had surged again to 17,000 by 1811 as ex-soldiers, Irish immigrants and dispossessed agricultural workers jostled side-by-side with established weavers for work. The middle-men, or 'piecers-out', were able to drive the work price down to such an extent that within six years of Horrocks's New

Prestoners' three-day week the weavers were living on or below the poverty line, and by 1808 were sending petitions of thousands of signatures to entreat Parliament to set a legal minimum wage. The bill was 'talked out' and the call for help ignored. In the face of this rebuff many embittered weavers took a cynical view of the anti-Napoleonic rhetoric of the patriotic 'Church and King' movement.

Between 1800 and 1810 there was an active resistance to the spread of machines and mills, especially among the textile workers of Lancashire and Yorkshire. The Luddites, as they were known, started off as spontaneous local brotherhoods, bound by oaths, signs and ceremonies which the government agents were unable to penetrate. Despite the difficulties of travel, soon they had forged links with each other to form a revolutionary network throughout the North and beyond. However, after the most serious violence in 1809–1813, which involved the use of firearms and militia, and many killed in attacks on mills, the magistrates were empowered to arrest many on mere suspicion. The movement faltered and disintegrated. By then the advance of the industrial age was irrevocable.

The ever-worsening conditions of the textile workers now began to awaken sympathy among men of conscience from all walks of life. During the next decade a political movement developed which sought to redress the problems through parliament and political means. This in turn needed an Act of Parliament to lower the qualifications for the right to vote, so that the social reformers' own candidates could be elected. The weavers and their champions turned to this 'Radical Movement' as their hope for a better life.

The Radicals introduced a new method of political expression the organised demonstration of popular support. These were peacefully conducted, but frequently were violently broken up by the authorities, who classed them as riots and sent in the militia. The greatest outrage was in Manchester in 1819. Leading

Continued on page 49

The Cockfight

Words: Verses from various sources (HBC, EBECS, PBEFS) with
modifications by Tom Walsh. Version of chorus from singing of Dave Peters,
Gypsy Wagon builder, Longton.
Tune: Re-arranged and adapted from above sources by Tom Walsh, 1989.

Come all you cockers far and near,
I'll sing of a cockfight, when and wheer
At Primrose Hill I heard 'em say
Between the black and the bonny grey.

   Chorus:
   With the silver breast and the silver wing
   He's fit to feight in front o't'king
   Hup and a Ha and a loud hooray
   We'll lay our money on the bonny grey.

It's in to the inn for to take a sup
The cockpit it is soon made up
Ten guineas a side each cock will play
The charcoal black and the bonny grey.

The first to come in were the Liverpool lads
They come with all the money they had
The reason why I heard 'em say
The black's too big for the bonny grey.

Lord Derby he come swaggering down
Sayin', 'I'll lay ten guineas to half-a-crown
If the charcoal black he gets fair play
He'll rip the wings off the bonny grey'.

And it's into the ring the cocks are tossed
Them Liverpool lads said, 'Now you've lost'.
Us lads had wagered all our pay
We wished they fought for a gallon of ale.

Now the cocks they at it with a one, two, three
The charcoal black got pecked in th'eye
They picks him up but he would not play
The fighting went to th'bonny grey.

This song has been collected in various versions all over the North West, modified to give local references. The verses here tell the basic story, similarly modified to a Preston context. The reference to the Earl of Derby occurs frequently. The 12th Earl, known as 'Sporting Stanley', was an inveterate gambler and a noted supporter of cock-fighting. He built a private cockpit next to the Bull Hotel in Preston in which to entertain his aristo-cratic fellow-enthusiasts. His son, very much a serious academic, turned it over to the Temperance Movement to use as their meeting-place and offices in 1830, and it was there that the Teetotallers ac-quired their new name (see 'Joseph Livesey'). One suspects that it was some time before the 12th Earl's body stopped rotating.

Left: A poster advertising race meetings held during the Preston Guild of 1822 with, at the bottom, notice of a match between Lord Derby's cocks and those of Mr. T. Legh.

Long after its Parliamentary ban cock-fighting continued to be popular in the town, though elaborate precautions had to be made to avoid the attentionsof the police:

'At a Preston meeting the mayor was one of the spectators. The sudden arrival of the police placed him in a predicament, so to escape he hid up the chimney. His girth prevented him from concealing himself entirely but the police, recognising the dignitary's nether regions, left him where he was.'

(A. Delgado, *Victorian Entertainment*, 1971.)

The Handloom Weaver's Lament
(Ye Tyrants of England)

Words: 'From the singing of John Grimshaw of Gorton', BSL (1866).
Tune: ibid, *A-hunting we will go.*

You gentlemen and tradesmen that ride about at will
Look down on these poor people, it's enough to make
   you chill.
Look down on these poor people as you ride up and
   down,
I think there is a God above who'll bring your pride
   quite down.

Chorus:
   You tyrants of England, your race may soon be run,
   You may be brought into account for what you've
      surely done.

You pull down our wages, shamefully to tell
You go into the markets and you say you cannot sell
And when that we do ask you when these bad times
   will mend
You quickly give an answer, 'When the wars are at an
   end'.

When we look at our poor children it grieves our
   hearts full sore
Their clothing it is worn to rags while we can get no
   more
With little in their bellies they to their work must go
While you dress as swanky as monkeys in a show.

You go to church on Sundays, I'm sure it's nowt but
   pride
There can be no religion where humanity's thrown
   aside.
If there be a place in heaven as there is in the Exchange
Our poor souls must not come near there; like lost
   sheep they must range.

With the choicest of strong dainties your tables are
   o'erspread
With good ale and strong brandy for to make your
   faces red
You call a set of visitors – it is your whole delight –
And you lay your heads together for to make our faces
   white.

You say that Bonaparte has been the spoil of us all
And that we have got reason for to pray for his
   downfall
Now Bonaparte is dead and gone and it is plainly
   shown
That we have bigger tyrants and Boneys of our own.

And now, my lads, for to conclude, it's time to make
   an end
Let's see if we can form a plan so these bad times
   might end
Then give us our old prices as we have had before
And we can live in happiness and rub off the old score.

The Handloom Weaver's Lament

Harland places the song as dating from after the battle of Waterloo. During the period 1805–1818 the handloom weavers plummetted from prosperity to semi-starvation and the first records of agitation in the cotton industry began. The last verse, with its hope for a restoration of the old balances between artisan and middleman, indicates that it predates the Peterloo Massacre of 1819, after which the tune was used for *With Henry Hunt We'll Go.*

The Luddites

Over a 400-year period an economic system had developed in England which by the 1780s gave employment to large numbers of labourers and artisans. While poverty, injustice and abuse still abounded, there was also interdependence, job satisfaction, and craft guilds with rules of apprenticeship and good practice. Machines played a part in most trades, but they were not the preserve of a few, and they existed to serve, not to rule.

The new class of machines, duplicating the work of many conventional craftsmen, made fortunes for their owners while driving down the product price. The fragile balance of local economies was shattered. Men whose families had spent generations in specialised trades saw the spectre of bankruptcy, eviction and starvation. Small wonder that threatening letters were sent to the new factory masters, and that masked gangs of men broke in to destroy their machines.

In many cases these attacks were semi-spontaneous, 'copycat' expressions of protest. However, there is no doubt that in some parts of the country – Lancashire, Yorkshire and Nottinghamshire especially – communication was established between Luddite groups, organisation was introduced and revolution discussed. It was not difficult to preach against an economy which was merely a part of a corrupt political system, geared to the support of a select minority by the majority. The recent successful overthrow of such systems in America and Europe was looked on with envy by many in England.

The government responded with a raft of repressive legislation supported by a flood of agents and spies. The working classes, bound in close-knit communities, were well able to prevent infiltration and to maintain an atmosphere of trust and secrecy. The widespread illiteracy assisted this secrecy, since meetings went unrecorded, instructions were memorised, and communications between groups were not written (which could have been intercepted), but verbal. Members recognised each other by secret signs and passwords, and were bound together by solemn oaths.

Attacks on machinery, still the most visible signs of the growing network and pressure, reached their peak between 1809 and 1813, when many deaths and injuries were caused in pitched battles between Luddite bands and millowners, especially in West Yorkshire. It has been said that England never stood closer to revolution than at this time, and yet a signal for concerted action never materialised. Maybe it never could. Meanwhile, the government, increasingly fearful, virtually created a police state in which 'sedition' (i.e. protest), 'combination' (i.e. opposition parties) and even 'oath-taking' became capital offences. Magistrates could now arrest on the slightest suspicion. Wholesale execution and transportation became commonplace. Deprived of its most articulate leaders, inevitably undermined by spies and paid informers, the Luddite organisation became inactive as a potential revolutionary force. Its members turned to the Radical Movement as a hope for redress. The spread of factories continued inexorably.

The surviving Luddites held true to their blood- oaths by taking their secrets to the grave with them. In consequence, hardly anything is known of the extent of their organisation and real aims, which remain a tantalising mystery to modern historians.

The established verdict on the Luddites promotes a picture of bands of brutish illiterates attempting to halt, by crude violence, the onward march of progress towards the golden age offered by the Industrial Revolution. That their name survives today only as a synonym for resistance to 'progress' represents a victory for William Pitt's propaganda machine, the myth being further perpetuated by the more simplistic history books.

Henry ('Orator') Hunt

Born in 1773 into a prosperous Wiltshire farming family, Henry Hunt grew to be a studious but high-spirited youth who in his twenties espoused Radical politics after experiencing the suffering of the poor of his district and the incompetence of the local authorities in relieving it.

In those days such administrative posts were obtained mostly by bribes or through the favour of aristocratic patronage, neither of which selection process took any account of actual ability. These 'pensioners' or 'placemen' often sought to divert the funds at their disposal to their own benefit, at the expense of the poor and sick. This 'Old Corruption' was one of the major targets of the Radical party.

Between 1797 and 1807 Hunt established himself as a contentious local politician, indulging freely and fearlessly in self-conducted lawsuits, and had in London been introduced to the leading radicals of the day. In 1811 he even shared a cell with reformer William Cobbett, and the two became friends for many years. By 1817 he had abandoned farming and was working full-time speaking for the Radical cause, supported by donations from sympathetic Radical committees and supporters.

He was soon counted as the leading public speaker of the Radical front, and his impassioned oratory drew roars from crowds of 20,000 and more, as he inflamed their desire for justice with calls to action that fell carefully just short of treason. A skilled self-publicist, he was always seen in public wearing a white hat, which became a symbol of Radicalism. He spoke at the great London Radical demonstrations at Spa Fields in 1817 and Smithfield in 1819.

On August 16th of that year he had just begun to address the great Manchester meeting at St. Peter's Fields when the Manchester Yeomanry attacked the crowd (the 'Peterloo Massacre') and he was arrested and imprisoned. At his trial he conducted his own fierce defence, but was sentenced to two years in Ilchester prison, and required to stand £2,000 of surety of future good behaviour. Flowers were strewn in front of the coach that took him to prison.

Medals and locket-portraits with his effigy were distributed to children in many Radical centres.

He now regarded himself as a great martyr to the cause (referring to himself as 'Saint Henry of Ilchester'), and his latent vanity appears to have got the better of him at this time. In prison he wrote his self-adulatory *Memoirs*, and adopted the title of 'the Champion of Liberty'. From then on he appears to have been generally disliked at a personal level for his arrogance by his Radical associates, while at the same time generally admired for his integrity, oratory and personal commitment to the cause.

After a highly publicised release from prison he temporarily adopted a low political profile and worked on various business ventures with limited success. Shares in a brewery were followed by the promotion of a new culinary concoction based on corn, roasted and ground, and marketed as 'Radical breakfast powder'. His final and most enduring business was as a manufacturer of boot blacking.

In August 1830 he threw his familiar white hat back into the political ring by standing as Radical candidate for Preston. On this occasion he was unsuccessful. However, when a second election was called in December, he gained the seat and made a grand entry into Westminster the following February as M.P. for the town.

His time in parliament was short and turbulent, for he attacked the programme of limited parliamentary reform as a betrayal of the aspirations of the working class, advocated the abolition of the infamous Corn Laws, and generally espoused a manifesto that was to take many years to come into being. Having lost the support of the pragmatists of his own party (he had long since lost their affection on account of his arrogance), he lost his Preston seat as a result of the reduced electorate.

He retired from politics to concentrate on his business interests and died shortly afterwards at the age of 62, suddenly, while travelling for orders. On his death a broadsheet elegy had considerable sales, and the example opposite is reproduced from the Harkness collection (Book 3, no. 38).

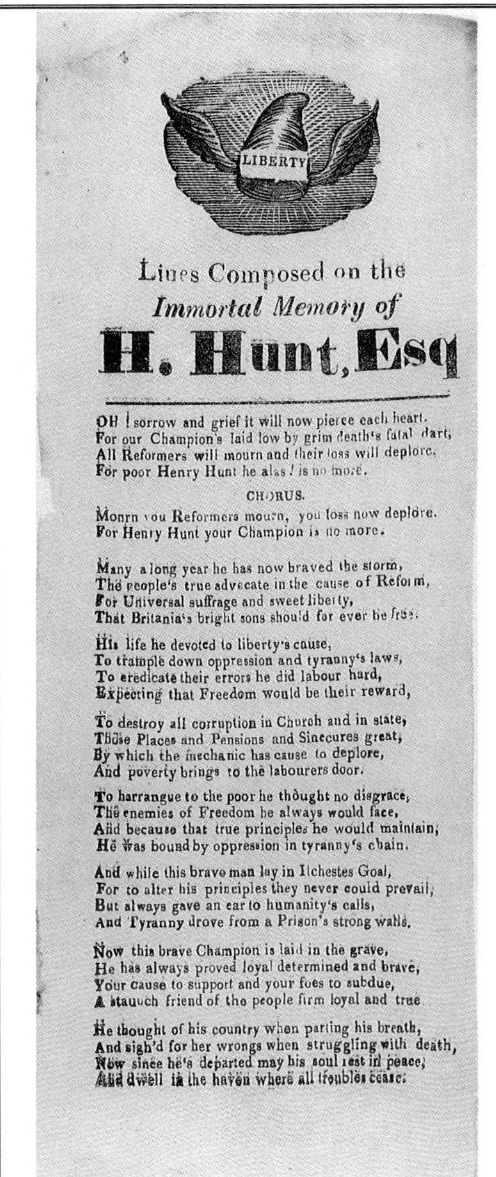

Radical orator Henry Hunt had just begun to address a crowd of many thousands of weavers from the North West at Saint Peter's Field when the local militia cavalry attacked the crowd with sabres. Many were killed and hundreds injured. This action against unarmed civilians acquired the derisive title 'The Battle of Peterloo'.

Local balladeer Michael Wilson was present and composed a song that very night, although not all the verses have survived.

A wave of national revulsion ensured that the militia were not used in this way again for many years. However, the lot of the weaver continued to worsen. Unable to combine together, desperate individuals in the over-crowded trade were forced by the unscrupulous warehouse masters to undercut each other just to afford to live in semi-starvation. There were few weaving mills in Preston at this time; the machines could not handle the trickier jobs as well as the hand-loomer. They were merely used as a threat against higher payment claims. In Preston the wages of the workers in the spinning mills were kept tied in with those of the weavers. Many strikes took place in the 1820s, but conditions improved little, and for many the workhouse marked the end of a short working life of hunger, debt and despair.

With the advent of the mills and the influx of weavers and millworkers, the Preston of the 1822 Guild was growing quickly. Wealthy owners built mansions in fashionable Winckley Square. For the weavers there were crowded, insanitary tenements off Friargate and other town-centre streets. For the mill-workers the same, or jerry-built terraced houses on the edge of town, riddled with damp and backing on to open sewers.

From the start, the cotton workers of the town had refused to be cowed into any easy submission. Agitation had been first recorded back in 1808 at the time of the weavers' petition. The handloom weavers had struck in 1818 as part of the process that led to Peterloo the following year. In 1821 it had been the turn of the workers in the spinning mills. In 1823 an assassination attempt was even made on the life of Samuel Horrocks (lethargic successor to his energetic brother's vast fortune) in protest at his wage levels. 1826 saw riot and machinery destruction all over Lancashire as the Radical Movement impatiently flexed its muscles in the Preston hustings.

Continued on page 53

The Peterloo Massacre

Words: SOTW 1866. Chorus modified (Tom Walsh, 1991).
Tune: ibid, identified as *Gee Whoa Dobbin*.

Come, Robin, sit down and I'll tell you a tale
But prithee first fill me a dobbin of ale
I'm as dry, mon, as soot and I'm hurt in me crop
And I left Sam o'Dick's where I fear he must stop.

>Chorus:
>For the Gentlemen Cavalry cut 'em down cleverly
>Jolly brave heroes, Gentlemen all.

Mr. Hunt now come forward to say a few words
When them Peterloo cut-me-throats shakened their swords
I thought sure enough they were running their rigs
Till I seed more'n twenty a-bleeding like pigs.

But let's take a peep at these Peterloo chaps
As makes such a noise about collars and caps
See what they're composed on and then we may judge
For it runs in me mind that their loyalty's fudge.

There's the taxman, exciseman, lawyer and bum,
Pensioner, placeman and preachers that hum
The fat-gutted landlord in license of fear
Cuts the throats of his neighbours that drink his bad beer.

The words were written by Michael Wilson (1767–1840), an Edinburgh Jacobin who moved to Manchester and doubtless witnessed the event. With heavy sarcasm he targets the 'patriotism' and 'courage' of the Militia Cavalry, most of whom were government officials who usually obtained their appointments through corruption and patronage and were naturally opposed to any reform. Only four verses survive; two are lost.

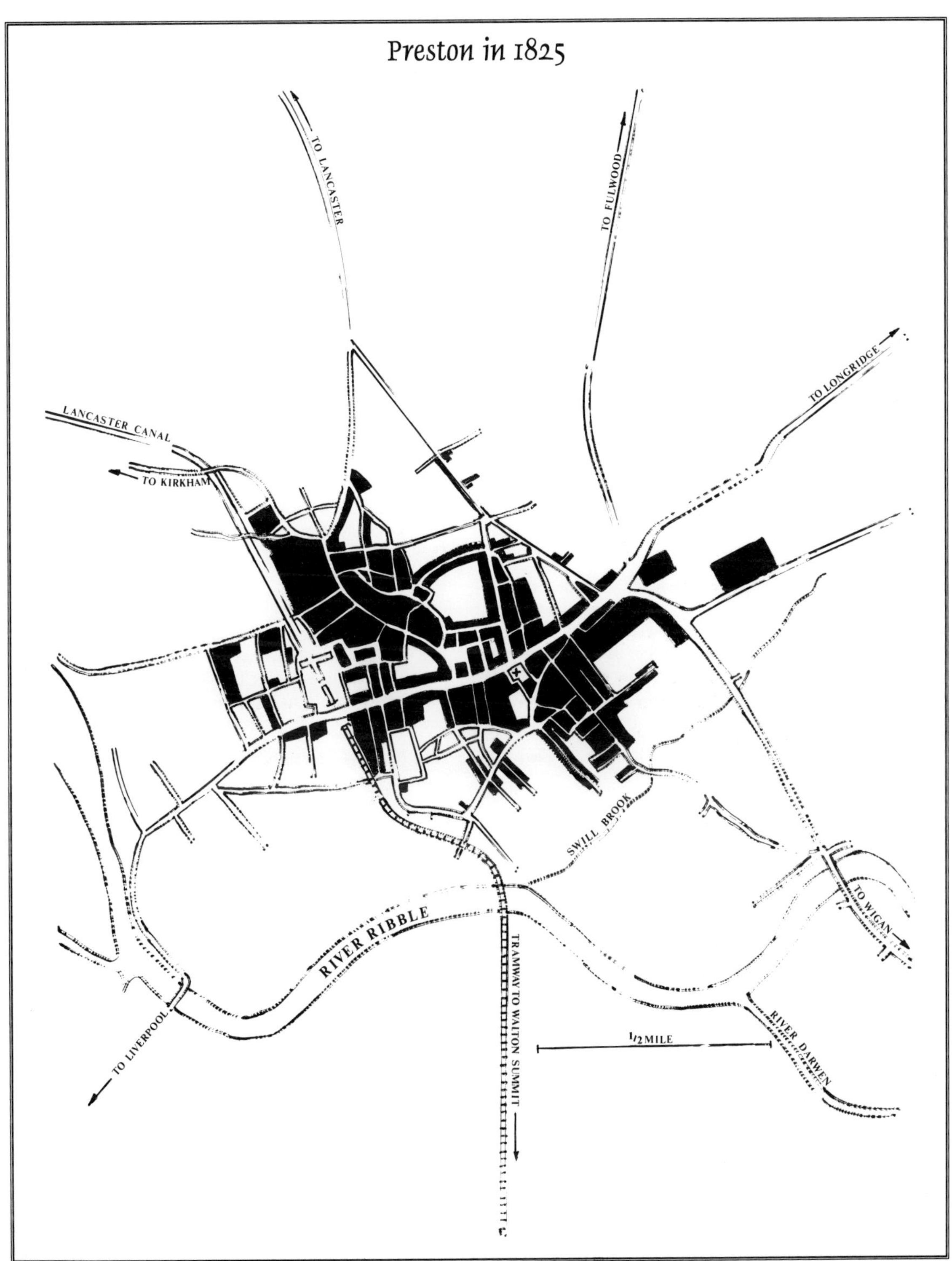

Preston in 1825
TO LANCASTER
TO FULWOOD
TO LONGRIDGE
LANCASTER CANAL
TO KIRKHAM
SWILL BROOK
TO WIGAN
RIVER RIBBLE
TRAMWAY TO WALTON SUMMIT
TO LIVERPOOL
1/2 MILE
RIVER DARWEN

Jon O'Greenfield Junior

Words: 'From the singing of a Droylsden man ... dates from 1816', BSL
(1866). Also HBC.
Tune: 'One of two versions collected by Frank Kidson in Cheshire', notated in
FSIE.

I'm a poor cotton weaver as many a man knows
I've got nowt to eat and I've worn out me clothes
Me clogs they are brozzen and stockings I've none
You'd scarce give us sixpence for all I've got on.
You'd think it were hard to get sent into th'world
To clem and do best as you con.

We held on six weeks, thought each day were the last
We stuck it six more and now we're stuck fast
We lived upon nettles when nettles were good
And Waterloo porridge were the best of us food
And I'm telling you true I know folks not a few
As are living no better'n me.

Our church parson kept telling us long
We should see better times if I'd just hold me tongue
Well, I've holden me tongue till I scarce can draw
   breath
In me heart I thinks that he'd fain clem me to death
He lives bloody well out of back-biting t'devil
But he ne'er had to weave in his life.

Old Bill o'Dan's sent in th'bailiffs one day
For a shop score I owed him that I couldn't pay
But he were too late, 'cos old Billy Bent
Had sent t'tattin cart and pinched all th'goods for
   th'rent
There was just an old stool that were seating for two
And on it cowered Margit and me.

Them bailiffs looked round as sly as any mouse
When they saw all the goods had been taken from
   th'house
Says one to the other, 'All's gone, tha mun see'.
Says I, 'Never fret, lad, tha's welcome to me'.
They made no more ado, they whipped up the old stool
And we both went whack upon th'flags.

Well I grabbed hold of Margit for her's stricken sick
Her said her's ne'er had such a bang since her were
   wick
Them bailiffs scoured off with wer stool on their backs
They would not have cared if they'd broken wer necks
They was mad at old Bent getting our stuff for rent
They was ready to flay us alive.

Well, I says to our Margit as we lay upon th'floor
'We shall never get lower in this life I'm sure.
And if things would but alter I'm sure they must mend
For I think to meself we're both at the far end
For yarn we have none, nor looms to weave on.
Eeh God, we're as well lost as found'.

Then I gathered me stuff and I took me piece back
I scarcely dared speak, master looked so black.
Says he, 'You were o'erpaid last time you come'.
Says I, 'If I was, t'were for weaving baht loom,
But mind as I'm in I'll ne'er weave again
I've woven meself to't far end'.

Then I went out o't'warehouse, left him to chew that.
The more I thought on it I were vexed till I swat
To think we mun work to keep him and his set
All the days of our lives and then die in their debt
Oh, I'll give o'er this trade – I'll work with a spade
Or go and break stones on the road.

Our Margit declares if she'd clothes to put on
She'd go up to London to see the great mon
And if things didn't alter once she had been
She swears she would fight, aye, blood up to th'een
She's nowt against king, but she likes a fair thing,
And she says she can tell when she's hurt.

Jon O'Greenfield Junior

Jon O'Greenfield is a mythical Lancashire folk-hero, a predecessor of Private Samuel Small and the Ramsbottom family of Bury. A series of dialect songs by various authors (including the Wilsons) survives from the first half of the nineteenth century, wherein events of the day are drily observed by this typical down-to-earth example of Homo Lancastriensis – an early version of the American *Talking Blues*. This song gives a heart-breakingly immediate picture of the realities of the hand-loomer's life at the bottom of the pile.

But in spite of growing national sympathy and support, the Radical Movement seemed unable to loosen the grip of the ruling classes over the legislative process. 'Catch-22' stopped them: there were not enough voters to vote in the M.P.s who would reform the system and so create more voters.

For many, hope began to turn into cynicism or despair. Small wonder that growing numbers sought relief in alcohol available in the myriad taverns and beer shops, old and new, which were proliferating throughout the town – especially once they were freed of licensing restrictions by an Act of Parliament in 1830. Soon Preston was notorious through-out the country for its level of drunkenness and drink-related crime.

In that same year of 1830 a local shopkeeper and Radical, Joseph Livesey, and some like-minded citizens decided to promote the benefits of abstinence. Scoring some well-publicised conversions of some – not all – of the town's better-known drunkards, the Temperance Movement spread quickly out from Preston and on through the country.

Four years later, in 1834, a general meeting of the society was held in the old town cockpit by then an assembly room after the sport's recent Parliamentary ban. The hot debate was whether the new pledge should mean absten-tion from spirits only, or embrace all alcoholic drink. In support of the latter spoke Dick Turner, one of their earliest successes. He had a curious habit of pronouncing the capital letters that handbills and ballad-sheets of the day used for emphasis. His speech in favour of 'Tee-total Abstinence' carried the day, and the movement continued to spread round the world under the new name provided by this citizen of its birthplace.

Not that the movement put local landlords out of business by any means. Preston people, then as now, continued to sup temperately, to excess, or not at all, as suited them. After all, it was said that in Preston there was no bad ale,'only degrees of goodness'!

In 1830 Preston, now boasting 33,000 inhabitants, once again became the nation's battleground, as the stage for the electoral showdown between the Radicals and the Reactionaries. Unlike anywhere else in the country, you could vote for Preston's two Members of Parliament if you were: (1) male; (2) had no criminal record; (3) were not a lunatic; and (4) had been resident in the town for six months prior to the election. In other words, it had universal male suffrage – incomprehensibly liberal for that day and age.

The reasons for this were partly due to the independent stance of its early guildsmen, but mostly to some political sharp practice in 1784 by the Derby faction, who had opened up the voting qualification for Preston by Act of Parliament to get their man elected. This liberalisation was now to backfire most unexpectedly.

The elections had been for years little more than a formality for voting in various Lord Derbys who provided free drinks for the voters

Continued on page 56

Joseph Livesey

Born March 5th 1794 in Walton-le-Dale, Joseph Livesey was orphaned at the age of seven and was subsequently brought up by his grandfather and uncle. His immediate employment was winding cotton onto bobbins for the three handlooms they operated in a cellar of their house hard by the banks of the Ribble; a cellar which was always cold, damp and sometimes even flooded.

After a while he graduated to weaving, and during this period he educated himself from books propped up against the shaft of the loom. He left the weaving trade when prices started to fall, and set up as a cheese merchant. By 1830 he was reasonably prosperous, with premises on Church Street, and employing a small workforce.

Prosperity did not make him forget the circumstances of his early years, and all his life he was a campaigner on behalf of the poor.

He campaigned against the Enclosures Acts of the early eighteenth century which caused widespread distress in country districts; against the harsh Poor Laws of 1834 and the hated workhouse system; and later against the Corn Laws which kept the price of bread artificially high, from 1841–46 producing a weekly newspaper called *The Struggle* at his own expense. For these political reforms he worked tirelessly.

When in 1830 the government introduced the Beer Acts, which reduced the restriction on the sale of beer, ale and porter, it believed that this would reduce the general drunkenness that was attributed to the availability of cheap gin, by encouraging the population to turn to the less alcoholic beverages. Unfortunately, it did not have the desired effect; it resulted in the proliferation of cheap drinking shops (196 opened up in Preston within two years), and more drunks.

Temperance societies had already been introduced to many towns by the Methodists. However, they advocated temperance rather than abstinence, forbidding spirits but not wine or beer.

In 1831 Joseph Livesey, a member of the Preston Society, decided that this ruling was too vague. He enjoyed an occasional glass himself, but decided that as an example to his workforce he would abstain from any form of alcohol. He soon became convinced that to persuade working men to abstain from alcohol would significantly improve their standard of living.

It was in 1831 that he embarked on this campaign of moral reform that was to become his life's work. He devised his 'pledge' of total abstinence and signed it along with five associates of the Preston Temperance League. He opened up a school for working men on Cannon Street, which became the centre of his move to persuade the league to commit themselves to total abstinence and abandon the 'moderation' doctrine. At the same time, his apostles crusaded through the town making increasing numbers of converts among the drinking population. Among them was the ebullient Dicky Turner.

By 1832 the full pledge was well and truly formulated, and at the first general meeting of the Preston Society it was accepted as part of the constitution alongside 'moderation'. This was not enough for Joseph Livesey. He kept persuading and lobbying so that by 1834 the 'moderation' option was abandoned and total abstinence became the only rule. It was at this meeting that the enthusiastic Dicky Turner coined the word 'Tee-total' (see main narrative) which was adopted by the society and entered the dictionary.

From then on until his death in 1886, Joseph Livesey and his followers travelled the country in the fervent promotion of Teetotalism, and the movement prospered. Not everybody was convinced by their arguments and they often encountered violent opposition, especially from the brewers. Nor were they above pulling a few tricks themselves in support of their cause. Nonetheless there is no doubt that many working people were able to find new purpose and a better quality of life through the zeal of Joseph Livesey.

'I hate a drunkard,' said someone once at a discussion on abstinence. 'On the contrary,' replied Joseph Livesey, 'I love a drunkard and I pity him from the bottom of my heart.' That statement is a significant insight into the humanity of the man.

Oh, Good Ale

Words: HBC, with extra verses collected by Tom Walsh from various sources.
Tune: Traditional

It's of good ale to you I'll sing
And to good ale I'll always cling
I likes me cup filled to the rim
I likes me nose stuck in the brim.

  Chorus:
    Oh good ale, thou art me darling,
    Though art me joy both night and morning.

I loves you in the early morn
I loves you daily, dark or dawn
And when I'm weary, worn and spent
I'll turn the tap and ease the vent.

It's you that helps me at me work
And from a task I'll never shirk
If I can get a good home brew
But better than one pint I likes two.

It's you that makes me friends me foes
It's you that makes me pawn me clothes
But soon as I gets thee to me nose
It's up thee comes and down thee goes.

And yes me wife does me despise
Last week she give me two black eyes
But if she loved me like I loved thee
What a happy couple we could be.

In comes the landlord, mighty big,
In a big black hat and powdered wig
In comes landlady, stout and fat,
Saying, 'Now, me lads, who'll pay for that?'

If all me friends of Adam's race
Were gathered here all in this place
I'd part from them without a tear
Before I'd part from thee, me dear.

Versions of this song are found all over the country. Home-brewed was in many cases much safer to drink than water and certainly more pleasant. However, it carried with it dangers of its own. The author of the song evidently sees himself as past any redemption.

E.G. Stanley, 14th Earl of Derby

While the polling was going on, the Hon. E. G. Stanley spoke out of one of the windows of the Bull Hotel, in Church Street, and he displeased the populace by saying that he was not going to be returned by the lower classes, or by those wearing fustian. They hissed him and the working classes turned against him.

'Afterwards, while going down Lune Street, he was set upon by the mob, back and front; and at the corner of Fleet Street he was thrown down, and spat upon, and shamefully abused. I was in my shop, saw him on the ground, went out and dragged him out of the gutter. They threatened to murder me. I got him into my shop, bolted the door and then, along with my wife, took him upstairs and hid him in a closet.

'The mob in the meantime were battering away at my door. They at length broke in and rushed into my shop. I ran into the back-kitchen and, pointing at the back door leading to Fleet Street, said, "Go that way!" And out they rushed, thinking that he had made his escape by that door and gone up into Fox Street.

When they had left, we told the gentleman to come out of the closet and, having done so, I and my wife washed him and cleaned his clothes. My wife was in a great state of alarm and cried; but he bade her not to do so; said that the mob would do her no harm; that it was him they wanted. Afterwards a couple of constables – they wore plain, ordinary clothes at that time – came and accompanied him along the bottom of Chapel Walks, past St. George's Church, through White Horse Yard and out into Friargate, and so on to the Bull Hotel. He was a tall, handsome, slender man, and they used to call him "Handsome Derby".'

Such was the tale of William Smith, Stanley's rescuer.

At the time of this unfortunate experience Edward George Geoffrey Smith Stanley, aged 31, Eton and Christ Church College, Oxford, had been an M.P. for eight years, the last four for Preston, and had been a junior minister (Under Secretary for the Colonies). Following his undignified defeat by Henry Hunt in December 1832, he quickly re-entered Parliament as M.P. for Windsor and subsequently for North Lancashire until 1844, when he joined the House of Lords, to become in 1851 the 14th Earl of Derby.

He was destined to a brilliant political career, always following his own course of cautious libertarianism, which required him to change sides from the Liberals to the Conservatives. He was Prime Minister in 1852, 1855, 1858–9 and 1866–8. He became much involved with the Irish questions of the day, frequently locking horns with Daniel O'Connell on questions of policy, though never losing the respect of the latter for his honesty. As Colonial Secretary in 1833 he carried the act for the abolition of slavery. He opposed the abolition of the Corn Laws and the demand for Free Trade.

As Prime Minister he supported Disraeli to pass the second great Reform Bill in 1867 which opened up the vote to all urban householders, and it is for this that he is chiefly remembered. In Preston he was more famous for his prodigious efforts towards the relief of distress during the Cotton Famine of 1861–64 caused by the American Civil War, which also did much to resotre the fortunes of the Conservative Party in the town. He died in 1869, and his commemorative statue can be seen in Miller Park to this day.

– more of a boozy carnival than serious politics. Now the Radicals, knowing the strength of support in the town, sought to gain their first M.P. They made several attempts during the 1820s and, in spite of various counter-moves, they got closer each time.

In 1830 it was the head-on collision. The reactionaries fielded Sir Edward Geoffrey Stanley, a Lord-Derby-in-waiting. The Radicals sent none other than Henry Hunt, the orator of Peterloo, now released from gaol and more fiery than ever. The drink flowed freely and so did the blood. Stanley insulted some millworkers and got a severe pasting. Even

Hunt got a smack on the nose from a cobbler for not being radical enough. But in the end, with the nation holding its breath, the result was declared . . . and Hunt entered Parliament as the first Radical M.P., representing Preston. In a state of considerable pique, Sir Edward Stanley abandoned his great house in the centre of Preston and never again lived in the town.

In 1831 another election was required. Hunt was returned unopposed. Together with other M.P.s sympathetic to the Radical cause, it was finally possible to pass the first great Reform Bill in 1832, which extended the vote to all men with a certain property qualification. The paradox was that Preston's unusual voting qualifications had now to conform with the improved national standard and became far narrower than before. Soon the old cabal was able to reassert itself. In 1835 prominent local landowner Hesketh-Fleetwood and another Stanley were elected again, and Hunt himself faded from the political scene.

Yet the Reform Bill did not bring about the dramatic changes that the poor had been expecting. Political change did not bring food and warmth to the weavers' hearths. Nor were the terms of the new Factory Acts always enforced. In any case, reduced hours in practice meant reduced wages. The political process was too slow to help the cotton worker bring up his family on his meagre wages. The infamous Corn Laws stayed in force, which kept the price of bread artifically high to protect farmers' profits. After so long pinning their hopes on the Radicals, many felt cheated. Yet they were told that they should be contented now that the reforms had been passed. Popular ballad-sheets soon began to deliver the working class's response to such condescension.

Amid all this turmoil Preston itself was continuing to grow quickly. By 1839, with a population of 46,000, it was now a centre for spinning mills. Some weaving mills existed – the handloom weavers were now almost all gone – but the main weaving centres lay to the east. The transport revolution brought by the new railway was sweeping the country, and Preston's position ensured that it rapidly became the centre of a rail network. Within six years it was connected to the south, the north, Manchester, Blackburn, Longridge, Blackpool, Southport and Liverpool, while the cuttings and viaducts became landmarks that have shaped the growth of the town ever since.

However, as a result of the failure of the Reform Bill to bring about real economic improvement at ground level, tempers were beginning to shorten. There was again a spinners' strike in 1836 which lasted into the following year. By the late 1830s Preston's M.P.s were only re-elected with the active support of 'cudgel-men', imported hooligans carrying clubs, who broke up rival meetings.

The Radical Movement now set about clarifying its aims. In 1836 it produced its Charter which set out six simple reforms to obtain equitable government: universal male suffrage; secret ballot; annual elections; constituencies of equal voter numbers; abolition of property qualification for M.P.s; and payment for M.P.s. A petition of 1.2 million signatures sent to Westminster failed to impress Parliament sufficiently to carry it through into law.

Though there was money to be made by a few, the average worker still lived and worked in appalling and dangerous conditions. The Cotton Masters' Association operated a cartel to obstruct any improvement that might diminish their profits or their grip on the town. No model factories here. Small wonder that support for the Charter was specially strong.

In fact, the general prosperity of the town probably suffered as a result of the fact that millworkers and masters were still of the same stubborn independent spirit – many of the cotton masters themselves came from the same artisan backgrounds. All the associated trades of an industrial, agricultural and railway centre were represented, plus ship

Continued on page 60

Forced to be Contented

Words: HBC; actually printed by J. Pannell, 24 Byrom Street, Liverpool.
Tune: Ron Flanagan, Longridge (1973), modified by Tom Walsh (1991).

You Britons all, where'er you be
I pray you listen unto me
And then with me you will agree
What makes us all contented.
The king is good, I mean to say
Because he cannot have his way
His brave men would not go astray
So we must be contented.

Chorus:
   Oh dear, oh dear, what times are these
   The rich will do just what they please
   The poor are starving by degrees
   And forced to be contented.

The rates and taxes are so high
All trades are ruined now or nigh
And the working class so fast do die
So we must be contented
This is the truth I mean to say
That England once looked fresh and gay
But now it's mouldering to decay
But we must be contented

The poor man he holds down his head
His children they are wanting bread
There's thousands starving still with dread
And are forced to be contented.
It is no use to talk at all
The weakest will go to the wall
And every day we lower fall
But we must be contented.

They said Reform would do us good
It has not yet, I wish it would
For thousands that are wanting food
Must starve and be contented.
The children to their fathers cry
As they for work are passing by
My belly's neither full nor nigh
So wander on contented.

The farmer cannot sell his wheat
The poor cannot get aught to eat
The world is ruined now complete
And forced to be contented.
The work is all now standing still
The next to stand will be the mill
All trades are fast gone down the hill
All hands must be contented.

The Reform Bill of 1832 did not have the dramatic effect on the conditions of the poor that they had been led to expect, for the reformers (against the advice of Henry Hunt, Preston's M.P.) had been forced to make too many compromises. The eventual realisation brought bitter disappointment, which in turn boosted support fo the Chartist movement.

The Coming of the Railways

The first railway in Preston was a horse-drawn tramway joining the two parts of the Lancaster Canal. This canal had been completed between Wigan and Walton Summit outside Preston, and from Preston across the Lune at Lancaster to Tewitfield north of Carnforth. These two sections were joined by the tramway in 1803, with the efforts of the horses being supplemented by winding engines on the steep inclines such as the one at Avenham. With the coming of the railways proper the days of the tramway were numbered, and the northern section to Preston closed in 1864.

The North Union Railway entered Preston from the south in 1838 opening up, by junction with other railway companies, communications to Liverpool, Manchester and the South of England.

The Lancaster and Preston Railway line from Lancaster reached Preston in 1840, terminating near the canal basin. A tunnel was constructed to join this line with North Union's Preston Station, but furious commercial rivalry broke out between the two railway companies, the canal company and, later, the Lancaster and Carlisle Railway. The disputes, one of which was so serious that Isambard Kingdom Brunel had to be called to adjudicate, raged until 1848 when various mergers incorporated all the protagonists and normal through-services to the North were established.

The line to Fleetwood was opened by the Preston and Wyre Railway and Harbour Company, opening in 1840 with its terminus at Maudlands and with a connection southwards on to the Lancaster line in 1844. For a while, this line provided the quickest route from the south to Scotland with railway travel to Fleetwood followed by a steamer to Ardrossan.

The Longridge Railway was built to transport stone from the quarries at Longridge to Preston and further destinations. The 6½-mile line was opened in 1840 with horse-drawn trains terminating at Deepdale Street. Steam arrived in 1848, and with it various grandiose plans to extend the line into Yorkshire. None of these came to anything, but the preparatory work at the Preston end was completed, with a link through to the Preston and Wyre Railway involving an 800-metre tunnel being completed in 1850. New stations were opened at Maudland Bridge and Deepdale, but direct access to Preston station was not achieved until a southward curve was constructed in 1885.

Longridge services terminated in 1967, though the line was kept open as far as the Courtaulds works at Red Scar until 1980. It currently terminates just south of Blackpool Road, and the original Deepdale Street terminus is still in use as a coal and oil terminal.

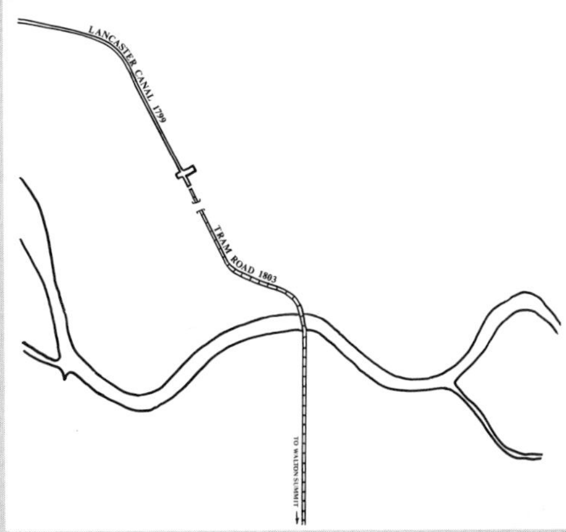

Above: The horse-drawn tramway system in c.1810.

Below: The railway system as it was at 1840.

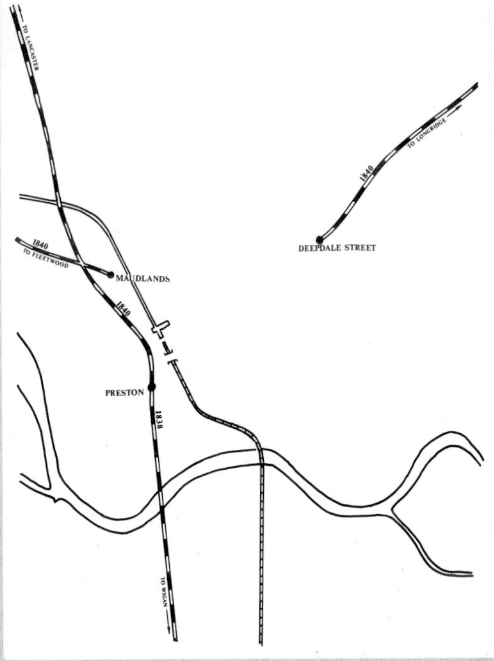

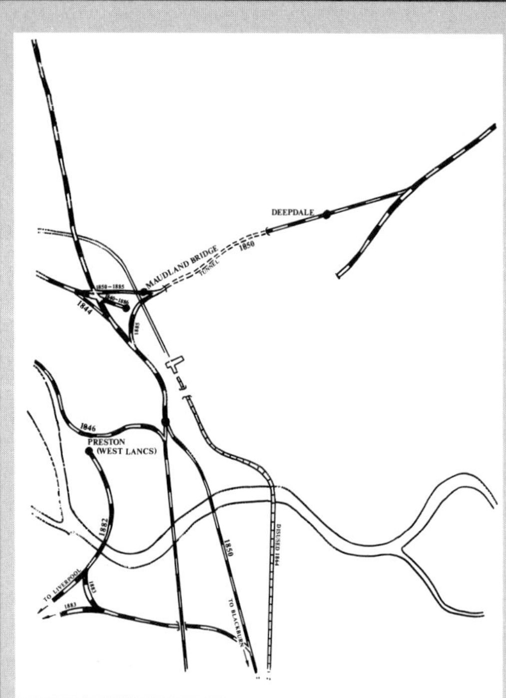

The railway system to 1890.

In 1846 a branch was opened from Preston station to the new Victoria Quay on the Ribble. This was later extended to serve the new Preston Dock on its completion in 1892. It features a 1:29 gradient, a tunnel, and a level crossing over Strand Road – and amazingly is still in use.

Rail connections with Blackburn and the rest of East Lancashire commenced in 1846, but access was difficult until the construction of the East Lancashire Railways 'Preston extension' line, crossing the Ribble between the tramway bridge and the main line, and entering the part of Preston station now covered by Asda's car park. This link also gave more direct access to Liverpool.

The last major expansion of the railway system in Preston was the opening of the West Lancashire Railway in 1882. This line from Southport terminated at the bottom of Fishergate Hill.

Its prosperity was always in doubt unless it could become part of a larger scheme, but the sought-after strategic alliances never materialised, and the Fishergate Hill station was closed to passengers in 1900 – though the line remained open until meeting the Beeching axe in 1964.

building on Ashton quays and the usual service industries and financial institutions, but the preponderance of cotton workers meant that the town's prosperity was always bound up with the prosperity (or otherwise) of the mills and the millworkers.

By the Guild of 1842 the mood nationally was ugly. On August 12th the Chartist leaders called for a general strike, and in Preston this was supported with enthusiasm. The factory hands issued from the mills, having first rendered the great mill engines lifeless by removing their pressure plugs. On the following day a large crowd of demonstrators proceeded into the town centre, singing the Chartist anthem as they marched.

On Fishergate they were to be met by the authorities in the form of the mayor, Samuel Horrocks, the town magistrates, the police, and a battalion of the 72nd Highlanders. The demonstration became violent as the crowd retreated down Lune Street and finally, in the vicinity of the Corn Exchange (later the Public Hall), the authorities suddenly found themselves surrounded. The soldiers opened fire on the crowd, killing or wounding about eight men. The stunned crowd quickly dispersed. To prevent further trouble, the authorities moved the Highlanders out and the Bolton Militia in that very night. News of the event spread round the country and much public sympathy was excited; even the Illustrated London News featured it.

In 1848, Europe's 'Year of Revolutions', the Chartists made a last attempt to promote their six points, but this, too, was unsuccessful. Its supporters now turned to trades unions and the co-operative societies as springboards to political change.

In 1853 the national spotlight again turned to Preston. Ten years previously, in response to a temporary slump in orders, the masters (who now liked to be styled 'The Preston Cotton Lords') had imposed a ten per cent reduction in pay rates. When trade improved the workers demanded that the old rates should

Continued on page 64

The Chartists' Anthem
(For All That)

Words: An anonymous adaptation of Robert Burns' *A man's a man for all that*.
Tune: The tune was probably composed at a later date to be used with Burns'
words, first appearing under that title in a book called
Merry Muses of Caledonia published in 1800.

Art thou, poor but honest man, sorely oppressed
  and all that?
Attention give to Chartist plan, 'twill cheer they
  heart, for all that,
For all that, for all that, though landlords gripe,
  and all that,
I'll show thee, friend, before we part, the rights
  of man and all that.

The right of man then's in the soil, an equal
  share and all that,
For landlord no-one ought to toil, 'tis imposition,
  all that.
Yes all that and all that, their title, deeds and all
  that.
Howe'er they got them matters not   the land is
  ours for all that.

Cursed be he who shall remove the poor man's
  bonds and all that
Or covet ought, should he improve his house or
  stock and all that.
Yes all that and all that, his cattle, goods and all
  that,
What God has gave all should enjoy and all the
  world should know that.

Then let us pray that come it may, as come it will
  for all that.
This Christian plan o'er all the earth shall be
  agreed and all that.
Yes all that and all that as come it will for all that,
That man and man the whole world o'er will
  brothers be for all that.

The Chartists had many songs to advocate their cause, very often adaptations of popular hymns.

The Shootings of Saturday 13th August 1842

In their brief descriptions of the dramatic events of 1842 the local chroniclers invariably adopt the conventional viewpoint in support of the millowners and against the operatives. This would have us believe that a vast mob damaged mill machinery, stoned police and the military and that the soldiers, surrounded by a rioting mob and in fear of their lives, fired upon the crowd causing the death of a small number and the streets to be cleared.

However, some clearer details of events emerge from transcripts of a subsequent political trial, where the Chief Constable of Preston, Samuel Bannister gave evidence for the prosecution of Fergus O'Connor.

The demonstration (referred to by conventional historians as the 'plug riots') was part of an organised, nationwide series of strikes in all branches of industry intended to support the Charter. The previous day in Preston, according to the pro-Chartist *Northern Star*, a mass meeting of Preston operatives had voted to go on strike 'until they had a fair day's pay for a fair day's work', and that 'before night every cotton mill was turned out without any resistance'.

To add to the political frustration there was an economic depression resulting in low wages and high prices for the basic necessities. Poverty, unemployment and malnutrition were everywhere to be found.

It should be remembered that in their campaign for the 'six points' the working people were actively supported by ministers of the Free Churches who added religious zeal to their aspirations and recognised that reform would not be achieved without strong-arm tactics in the face of the current political intransigence. The Free Churches preached that 'all men were equal in the sight of God'. The Anglican and Roman Catholic Churches, on the other hand, actively or tacitly supported the acceptance of the division of the world into rich and poor.

For this reason, Chartist meetings resembled religious services as well as political meetings, hymns and zealous sermons being integral to the proceedings.

Instead of turning up for work on the Saturday, a large demonstration was set in motion. One mill, Sleddon's on North Road, had to be persuaded, against some resistance from staff with hose-pipes, to join the strike. The demonstrators then congregated at Chadwick's Orchard (an open area near the present covered market and a regular assembly point for these events) and set off on a march round the town, led by the women and children.

The demonstration set off at about 8.00am out on to Friargate, up Lune Street and left on to Fishergate in the direction of the town hall. Opposite the Shelley Arms (now the site of Woolworths) they were met by the Mayor, Samuel Horrocks, the Chief Constables of Preston and Lancashire, Bannister and Woodford, sixteen policemen and thirty soldiers of the 72 Highlanders with muskets and bayonets spread across the road. With magistrates and other officials, they numbered about eighty.

It would appear that proceedings became ugly very quickly. The Riot Act was read and the demonstrators replied with a volley of stones evidently carried in the aprons of some of the girls and stockpiled at the end of Chapel Walks (opposite Winckley Street on Fishergate).

The troops now advanced and the crowd withdrew down Lune Street. The women and children had long since been withdrawn from harm's way and the crowd was headed by young male millworkers. As the authorities' force reached the corner of Lune Street and Fleet Street they found themselves trapped. A portion of the

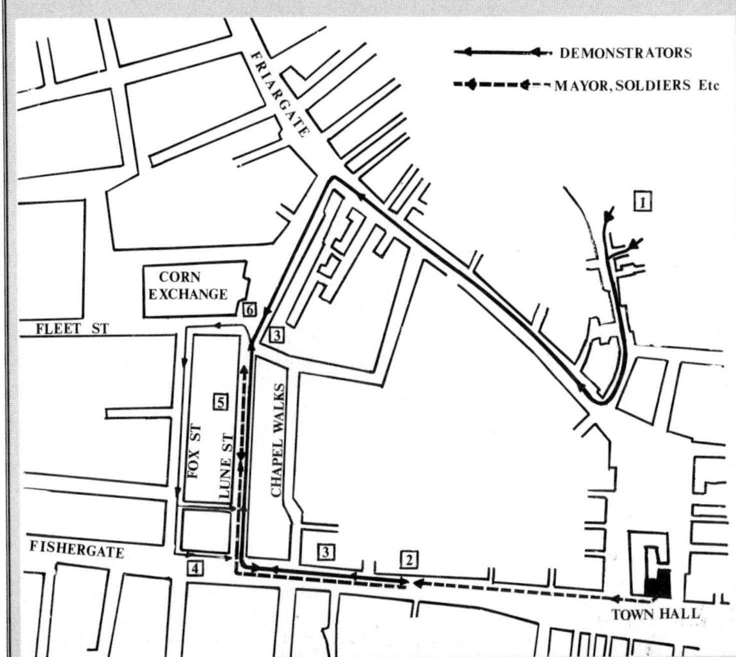

Left: The incidents leading up to the shooting of the demonstrators outside the Corn Exchange.

1. Demonstrators assemble at Chadwick's Orchard and march via Friargate and Lune Street to Fishergate.
2. Mayor, soldiers etc. from Town Hall confront crowd in Fishergate. Riot Act read.
3. Crowd retreat to Corn Exchange, followed by Mayor and soldiers.
4. Portion of crowd doubles back via Fox Street and blocks the Fishergate end of Lune Street.
5. Mayor, soldiers etc. cut off in Lune Street.
6. Soldiers fire into the crowd outside the Corn Exchange.

crowd had doubled back round Fox Street and Fishergate and blocked Lune Street behind them, although it did not resist a party of Royal Engineers (who were engaged in Ordnance Survey work based in Winckley Street) from joining the main body. In addition, some of the demonstrators had climbed up the scaffolding on the front of the Corn Exchange (later the Public Hall), where decoration and refurbishment for the forthcoming Guild was being conducted, and were lobbing bricks and stones from this vantage point.

The *Northern Star* reports that the policemen were running out from the ranks of the soldiers, striking the boys with their staves and retreating again. The soldiers, it would appear, were standing ground facing up and down Lune Street, muskets already loaded, protecting the hit-and-run tactics of the police. There was no attempt to defuse the situation by talk, and the soldiers were not ordered to march on the crowd. Presumably the Mayor and Magistrates wished to retain their protection.

At some point the Mayor was seen to speak to the Captain of the soldiers. At that point the firing commenced. Not a volley over the heads of the crowd, but a succession of single shots, about one every three seconds over the course of a minute, all in the direction of the Corn Exchange. Some shots hit surrounding buildings, other found their mark in the crowd itself (we cannot guess which were by accident and which by design).

'The mob stood mute; they did not attempt to run; they stood for some minutes as if thunderstruck . . . Four died ultimately and a fifth who was wounded had his leg taken off' (Bannister's evidence). In fact, Bannister would not answer a subsequent question of whether the firing continued even when the crowd was standing 'mute and thunderstruck'.

This was the end of any further demonstration. The dead and wounded were taken to hospital; the final toll would appear to be eight, but there is some dispute. The crowd dispersed and the normal bustle of a Saturday was replaced by a silence 'like to a Sunday'. There was a 'unanimous opinion among the working people that the Mayor ought to be tried for murder,' said the *Northern Star*. However, in fact, Horrocks received a vote of thanks from the citizens (the wealthy ones, at any rate).

As for the Highlanders, they were marched out under cover of darkness, to be replaced by the Bolton Militia that same night. For many years after that Scottish soldiers were shunned in the town. This was the last instance of civilian fatalities at the hands of the military in England. It is ironic, in view of all the Scottish blood spilt around Preston over the proceding two centuries, that a platoon of Highlanders was involved.

Sources:
Hewitson, *History of Preston*
Preston Chronicle
Northern Star
M. Jenkins, *The General Strike of 1842*

be restored, but the owners, headed by Thomas Miller, now responded jointly by closing all the town's mills. The 'Great Preston Lockout' (a new word coined by Miller himself) had begun.

However, the crowded conditions of mill work had now long since fostered unions and political discussion, communications and co-operation, so this new generation of strikers was able to rely on support and contributions from fellow workers and enlightened men and women all over the country. 'The eyes of the world are on Preston in Lancashire,' wrote Eliza Cooke at the time, 'where a titanic struggle is taking place between the forces of Capital and Labour.'

Representatives and flying columns used the new railways to visit local towns to address supportive audiences and gather contributions, often by selling ballads printed by Preston's own ballad-printer, John Harkness.

Able leaders came to the fore who could talk, like George Cowell, calmly and persuasively, or like Mortimer Grimshaw who roused crowds with embittered passion. Journalist Charles Dickens was dispatched to the town to report on this new phenomenon of worker solidarity, and used the opportunity to cull material for his next bestseller *Hard Times* while residing in comfort at the Bull Hotel. Neither side would give way, and the strike lasted on through the winter. A campaign of rumour and scandal was initiated against the strike leaders. When this failed, they were arrested on contrived charges. Gradually, inevitably, the financial support could no longer be maintained, and finally the Preston mill-workers returned to work. They had gained a new pride in their solidarity in what was the first nationally-supported strike, but little else.

The disappointments at the eventual outcome of this struggle which had started with such optimism left the workers demoralised. Not so the cotton masters who now, by

Harkness

John Harkness is, and presumably will forever remain, a shadowy figure known only by his prolific work. He was a stationer, printer and – pre-eminently – a ballad-publisher who, for much of the nineteenth century, carried on his business in Preston.

He produced well over 1,000 ballad sheets, which were sold on street corners and in the market by ballad-mongers who would sing snatches of their wares to attract the customers. In those days before radio and television, and when the newspapers had barely touched the bulk of the population, these ballad sheets were avidly bought as a prime source of news, scandal and simple entertainment.

Harkness appears to have started publishing from an address in Manchester Road round about 1838 and moved, via two addresses in Church Street, to North Road. His very last publications are from Howick and Longton, and it would appear that he lived in semi-retirement in Longton before his death some time in the late 1880s.

Harkness, Printer, Church Street, Preston.

Continued on page 66

TO M. MOORE.

By J. H., OCTOBER 7, 1841.

Thy soft, and kindly smile,
Has sooth'd my tortur'd mind,
And I have thought the while,
'Twere well thou couldst be kind.

For what had I e'er done for thee,
To merit thy esteem,
Yet thou hast ever been to me,
As friend to friend has been,

'Tis true thou saw me wither,
And perchance thou heard me sigh,
And thou griev'd, as would a brother,
That a tear should dim my eye,

So in return for thy esteem,
With fervency, and zeal,
I hold a generous sentiment.
Which I would now reveal,

We are childern of sorrow,
I have told thee half my woe,
We have promis'd on to-morrow,
To spend an hour or so,

In reciting tales of anguish,
To relieve each other's care,
For with thee I scarce could languish,
Though dealing with dispair.

Were I spirit discontented,
Were I sprite from burden free,
Were I faded to a vapour—
And could think—I'd think of thee,

And also were I with thee,
When thy cheeks are pale in death,
Then most fervently I'd bless thee,
Though silent were thy breath.

Were I bound within a desert,
My poor Muse of the would sing,
And with—mayst thou e'er be happy—
The desert wild should ring!

49

One of his last ballad publications was the Guild Song of 1882, reproduced in this book, and the last known reference to him is a listing as a stationer in Longton in the 1885 Preston Directory. He does not appear in any electoral or poll registers, nor is he included in the Guild Rolls of 1842, 1862 or 1882. The 1880 Preston Directory lists a Harkness, John, Jnr., as a printer in Gleswick Street, so it does appear that Harkness had at least one child and that he followed in his father's footsteps. This did not, unfortunately, save the bulk of Harkness' output. At his death most of his stock and printing materials were transported to Blackburn and sold for a pittance. It is said that many of his old publications were disposed of for waste paper.

For the fact that any ballads survived, we are indebted to various collectors who recognised early enough what interest the ballads, sitting as unconsidered trifles in libraries and bookshelves across the country, would have for the people of the new age.

In particular, Preston owes a debt of gratitude to Mr. J. H. Spencer, who started collecting Harkness broadsides around 1920 and built up a tremendous collection of over 1,700 street ballads including examples of 150 different Harkness ballads. Another source of Harkness ballads is the Madden collection. This compilation of 30,000 songs and ballads was the undertaking of Sir Frederick Madden of Leamington, nineteenth-century scholar and archaeologist. Madden served as keeper of manuscripts at the British Museum from 1837 to 1866 and, through auctions, private sales and regular contact with broadside printers, amassed the vast collection which now resides at Cambridge University. The fact that this collection contains upwards of 350 Harkness ballad sheets (some of which have been used in this book) testifies to Harkness having a national as well as a local significance.

Perhaps the only insight to Harkness the man is contained in ballad sheet number 49 of 1841. This is a poem of thanks and appreciation to 'M. Moore'. We reproduce it here but feel it does nothing to undermine the conviction that Harkness' main vocation was as a printer!

So what were the ballads like? They were single sheets of paper somewhere between quarto and A4 in size (though a couple of Harkness 'special editions' measure 24 x 16 inches), and were generally on fairly flimsy paper which has unfortunately not helped their survival. They were in a two-column format, so that the sheets could be cut in half and the halves sold separately. The range of material was very large, with old traditional ballads mixing with quality poetry and classical song. At the other end of the scale were contemporary popular songs, some of which show an absence of quality every bit as marked as any offering that the twentieth century has thrown at us.

Many of the ballads are headed by an illustration, but whereas most seventeenth- and eighteenth-century ballad sheets were careful to match the illustration with its subject, many of Harkness' offerings show no such inhibitions. Though Kitty of Coleraine (218) shows a loving couple walking, and cuts of Nelson and Napoleon almost invariably occur in the right places, we also have two beehives accompanying a drinking song (114), a humorous soldier figure adorns a highwayman ballad (265), and a couple at peace outside their cottage is hardly a fitting headline for the St. Helens Colliery explosion (604).

But, like any other medium, where there is some dross there are also nuggets of sheer excellence. Above all, the ballads convey a feeling of ordinary people and ordinary lives in the nineteenth century with an immediacy unmatched by anything else they have left behind. This is what makes a trip through the Harkness collection such a rewarding experience, and why Preston in general, and this book in particular, is so indebted to Preston's ballad printer.

buildings were begun at this time. The Parish Church was virtually rebuilt in 1855. The Town Hall, designed by Sir George Gilbert Scott, was commenced in 1862. To celebrate their new freedom to build churches, the Catholics in 1855 erected St. Walburge's to the designs of Joseph Hansom, who was also the designer of the Hansom Cab, first seen in Preston in 1868.

In 1861 another event occurred which was also destined to give Preston a certain world-wide notoriety. At the new Fulwood Barracks a Private McCaffery, embittered at victimisation at the hands of Adjutant Hanham, aimed a shot at him which killed both Hanham and the garrison commander, Colonel Crofton, who was standing at Hanham's side. McCaffery was duly hanged in 1862, but a ballad circulated to commemorate the event became popular in the barrack rooms, not least for its protest against the frequently ferocious treatment of soldiers by officers. Wherever the army went this Preston song went too – though to be caught singing it was said to be a punishable offence. It is still known by soldiers to this day.

1861 heralded worse trials still to come for the hard-pressed textile workers. The American Civil War began and the Union's blockade of Confederate ports meant that the cotton supply abruptly ceased. All the Lancashire towns suffered greatly in what came to be known as the 'Cotton Famine', but none more so than Preston, for the simple reason that it relied so heavily on the spinning trade. Weaving towns were able to obtain some spun yarn from outside, or adapt temporarily to wool or other yarns, but Preston needed raw cotton, and there was none to be had.

The Guild of 1862 was celebrated with such enthusiasm as could be expected under the circumstances. While its population had nearly doubled to over 80,000 since the last Guild in 1842, 23,000 townspeople were already on Poor Law relief and that number was still rising. Preston's erstwhile M.P., Edward

comparison, felt fully confident in their position. Money was readily available to support public building and similar enterprises on a grand scale, and many of the town's finest

Continued on page 71

George Cowell

George Cowell, who is the most popular of the leaders, is a striking personage in his way. He is rather under middle height, of a sallow complexion, has clear, open, mirthful eyes, breadth of forehead and a spirit of resolute, adventurous determination that makes him the master at once of the sympathies of his audience. He speaks in the broad dialect of the county, uses the idioms of his class with a consciousness of the force he gains by so doing, and stems opposition by the good-humoured decision by which he puts aside all objections. He chooses his words well and is in short one of the most effective popular orators I have seen.'

So wrote Henry Ashworth in 1853, one of the many journalists who visited Preston to report on the new phenomenon of an entire town locked in industrial conflict, a workforce determined to stick together and supported by fellow-workers in surrounding towns – indeed, throughout the country.

Ten years previously the owners had responded to a slump in trade by reducing wages by ten per cent; five years later the reduction was repeated. Now, in response to an upturn, there was a general demand for a ten per cent increase. A strike commenced in September of 1853 at Birley's mill on Great Hanover Street; the operatives began to receive support from fellow-workers in other mills. The owners, seeing that they might be picked off one by one, declared that until the demand was withdrawn they would close all the town's mills. As a result over 25,000 workers were put on to the streets with no means of earning a living.

Contributions to assist the operatives were now received from fellow-workers and trade unions in other towns. From Blackburn alone the vast sum of £18,845 was collected over the course of the lock-out. All money was logged by a committee of workers' leaders (the 'Operatives Executive') headed by George Cowell and based at the Temperance Meeting Rooms, and distributed by them for the relief of distress. More money was collected by groups of workers who used the railway system to visit towns and cities singing and selling 'lock-out songs'.

Through Cowell's careful administration of funds, his oratorical powers and his sheer leadership the worker solidarity held fast through to the new year and beyond with no sign of weakening. The owners attempted to ship in numbers of Irish immigrants to work the mills, but the success of this ploy was limited. They also initiated a smear campaign against the Operatives Executive, suggesting that they were spending fund money on themselves. This, too, met with limited success, given the respect in which George Cowell was held.

However, by the end of March 1854 tempers were getting short. There had been some instances of attacks on the immigrant Irish strike-breakers who, to be fair, mostly had no idea of the situation into which they had been introduced. These attacks gave the owners their opportunity and on March 24th Cowell and the rest of the committee found themselves under arrest for 'conspiracy to molest workers', and imprisoned.

Without the executive the resistance began to crumble and by April the workforces had returned to the mills on the owners' terms. It was August before George Cowell and his committee were brought to trial in Liverpool. The lock-out was by now just a memory and the judge acquitted them, bidding them to work hard; 'For by industry you may yourselves become masters'.

Further tribulations were still in store for George. The funds had been fully distributed and accounted for, but a printer's bill was outstanding. There was no money to pay, and he was thrown into Lancaster Castle as a debtor. Eventually the money was raised by public appeal and he was released. There was, needless to say, no possibility of employment for him in Preston and he moved to Manchester.

The efforts and stresses of leadership during the lock-out, the fund administration, the committee work and the hardship of the poverty a millworker had to endure would have taxed all the strength and powers of a man in his prime. It is amazing to discover that George Cowell, born in Balderstone in 1786, was 66 years old when the lock-out began. A former handloom weaver, he had seen the brief zenith and the long decline of that trade. Now a millworker, his robustness and resilience can only be marvelled at.

In fact, he remained active in Manchester for many more years, working full-time for Joseph Livesey's Temperance Movement, exercising his speaking and organising skills. In June of 1880, at the age of 94, having presided over the planning meeting for a new campaign, he suffered a stroke on Manchester Victoria station and died two days later without recovering consciousness.

A remarkable man indeed.

The Cotton Lords of Preston

Words: Harkness broadside ballad in the Madden collection.
Tune: Identified on the broadside itself as *The King of the Cannibal Isles*,
A.W. Humphreys, *circa* 1830.

Have you not heard the news of late
About some mighty men so great
I mean the swells of Fishergate
The Cotton Lords of Preston
They are a set of stingy blades
They've locked up all their mills and shades
So now we've nothing else to do
But come a-singing songs for you
So with our ballads we've come out
To tramp the country round about
And try if we can't live without
The Cotton Lords of Preston.

   Chorus:
   Everybody's crying shame
   On these gentlemen by name
   Don't you think they're much to blame
   The Cotton Lords of Preston

The working people such as we
Pass their time in misery
While they live in luxury
The Cotton Lords of Preston
They're making money every way
And building factories every day
Yet when we asked them for more pay
They had the impudence to say
'To your demands we'll not consent
You get enough so be content'
But we will have the Ten Per Cent
From t'Cotton Lords of Preston

Our masters say they're very sure
That a strike we can't endure
They all assert we're very poor
The Cotton Lords of Preston
But we're determined every one
With them we will not be done
For we'll not be content
Until we get the Ten Per Cent
The Cotton Lords are sure to fall
Both ugly, handsome, short and tall
For we intend to conquer all
The Cotton Lords of Preston

So men and women all of you
Come and buy a song or two
And assist us to subdue
The Cotton Lords of Preston
We'll conquer them and no mistake
Whatever laws they seem to make
And when we get the Ten Per Cent
Then we'll live happy and content
Then we'll dance and sing with glee
And thank you all right heartily
When we gain the victory
And beat the Lords of Preston.

The Cotton Lords of Preston

This is the classic fund-raising song from the early, optimistic days of the Preston Lock-out. The breezy tune was always a local favourite and is used for several other ballads of the time, including a couple from Harkness.

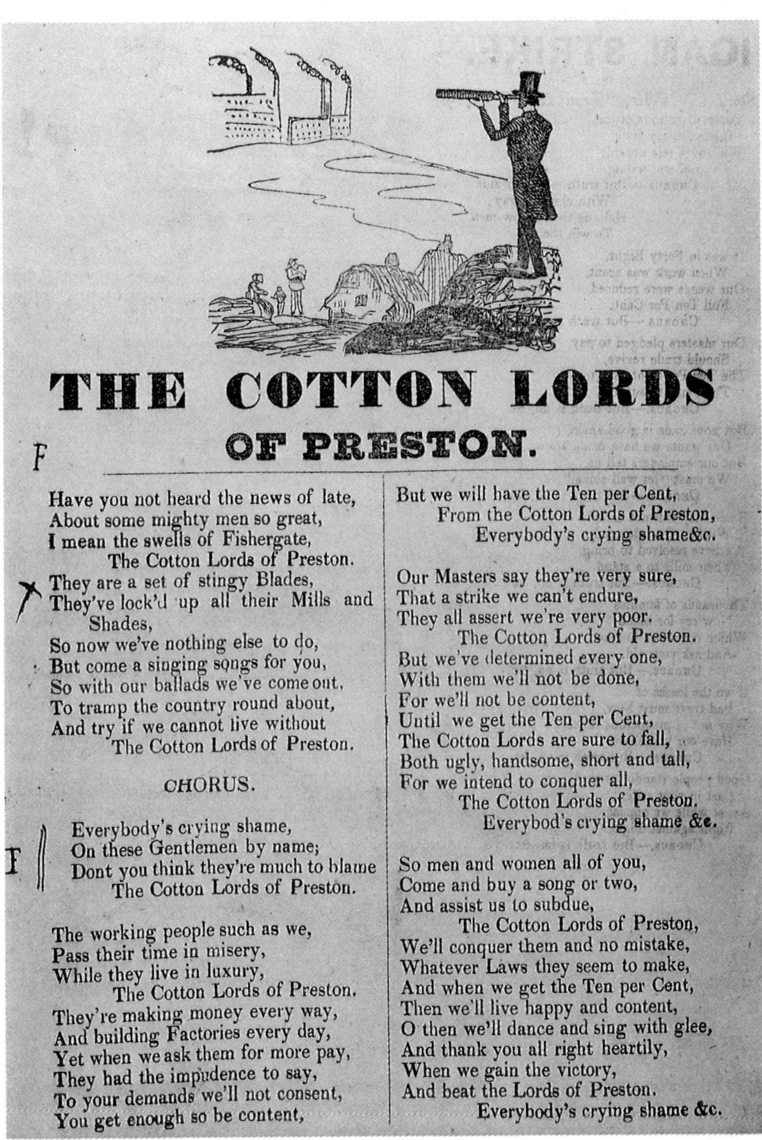

The original Harkness ballad sheet of *The Cotton Lords of Preston*: Madden Collection 18:1312.

Preston in 1865

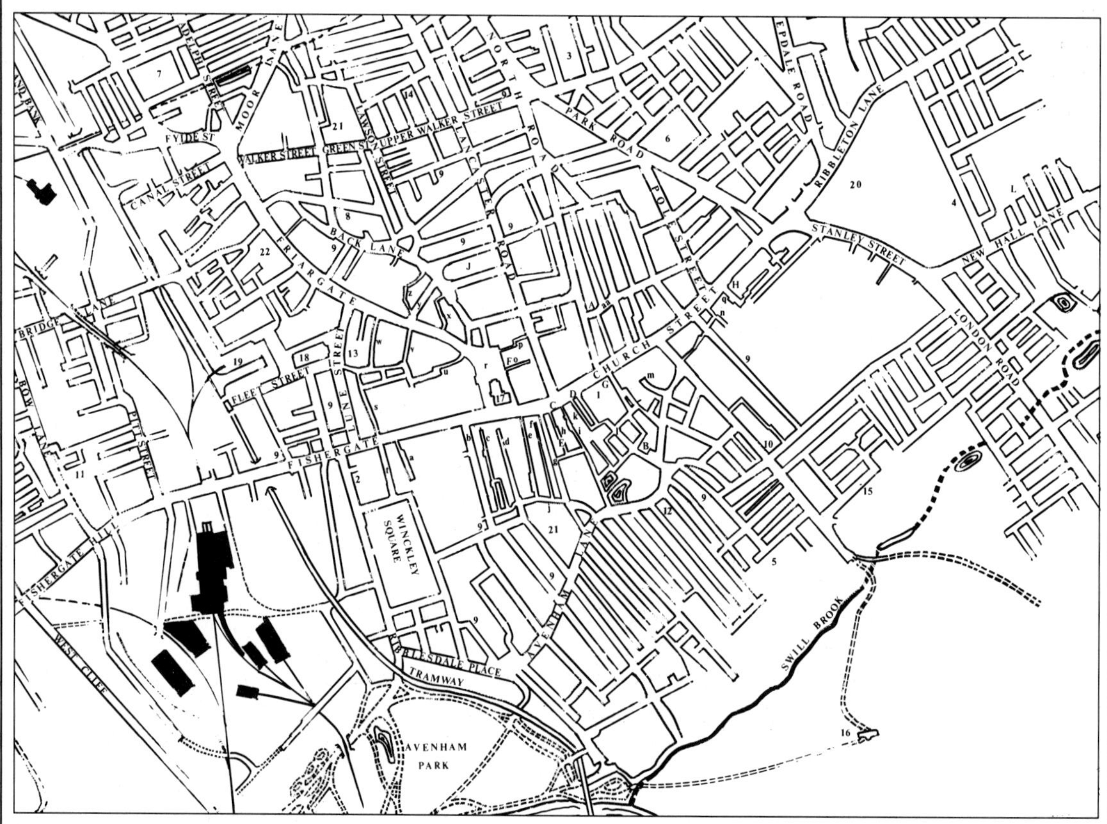

Key

1.	Parish Church, St. John's.	21.	Gas Works.	r	Market Place.
2.	St. Wilfred's Church.	22.	St. Mary's Church, Friargate.	s	Chapel Walks.
3.	St. Ignatius Church.	a	Butlers Court.	t	Winckley Street.
4.	St. Mary's Church.	b	Common Street.	u	Anchor Court.
5.	St. Augustine's Church.	c	New Cock Yard.	v	Bambers Yard.
6.	St. Paul's Church.	d	Glovers Court.	w	Mellings Yard.
7.	St. Peter's Church.	e	Main Sprit Weind.	x	Fishwick Yard.
8.	Trinity Church.	f	Old Cock Yard.	y	Orchard Street.
9.	Chapel.	g	Avenham Street.	z	Platts Court.
10.	St. Saviour's.	h	Turks Head Yard.	aa	Lord Street.
11.	Christ Church.	i	Boltons Court.		
12.	St. James's Church.	j	Syke Street.		
13.	St. George's Church.	k	Craystock Yard.		
14.	All Saints Church.	l	Stoneygate.		
15.	Larkhill Convent.	m	Old Dog Yard.		
16.	Frenchwood House.	n	Blue Bell Yard.		
17.	Town Hall.	o	Straight Shambles.		
18.	Corn Exchange.	p	Gin Bow Entry.		
19.	Canal Basin.	q	Cotton Court.		
20.	Prison.				

A   Lord Street, Arkwright's birthplace.

B   Arkwright House (originally the Grammar School), where Richard Arkwright built his first water frame.

C   The Grey Horse, Henry Hunt's election headquarters.

D   The Bull Hotel – Cockpit (Teetotallers' meeting place) and E. G. Stanley's election headquarters. Preston Grasshoppers RFC formed at a meeting here in 1869.

E   Turks Head Yard, site of Horrocks's first workshop.

F   Site of the Mitre Inn – surrender of the Jacobites in 1715.

G   The Parish Church, barricade and position of cannon during 1715 battle

H   Site of Joseph Livesey's shop.

I   Site of 1842 shootings.

J   Chadwick's Orchard, gathering place for demonstrations including 1842.

K   'New Preston', Horrocks's major manufacturing development.

George Stanley, Lord Derby, now one of the most prominent politicians of the day and a leader of moderate Conservatives, won great respect even among the Radicals for his tireless efforts to relieve the distress of the town. Soup kitchens were set up; welfare schemes were introduced; programmes of road building were initiated. However, in spite of the hardships, the cotton workers appear to have supported the Union intention of abolishing slavery. There was no outcry for the navy to escort Confederate cotton cargoes, although the Ashton shipyards of Mackern & Co. did build an ironclad steamship called the Night Hawk for the Confederate navy. Over two hundred feet long, it was launched in 1864 but was chased and sunk on its maiden voyage by the USS Niphon and never made Charleston.

The end of the war restored the cotton supply and the old quarrels. 1869 saw a nine-month spinners' strike, and 1876 the second Great Cotton Lockout when the now well-established trade unions first initiated a policy of selected targets (foiled by the employers closing all mills irrespective of whether they were involved or not). Once again there was much violence and no real winners on either side. However, by this time many of the greatest malpractices had been done away with by a Parliament which had been further moderated by the 1867 Reform Bill passed by Disraeli under the Prime Ministership of none other than Edward George Stanley, Lord Derby.

The period after the Cotton Famine also saw the completion of more familiar landmarks. English Martyrs was designed by Edmund Welby Pugin and sited on Gallows Hill where the 1715 Jacobite sympathisers had been executed. The County Offices were completed in 1882 and the first planning meetings for the erection of the new Penwortham bridge took place.

By the Guild of 1882 there was an atmosphere of optimism and merriment, to judge by the advertising at any rate. The town's popu-

Continued on page 77

Chronology Of Distress And Strife In The Preston Cotton Industry During The Nineteenth Century

for which the town acquired the title of
'The chief battlefield
of the Lancashire Cotton Industry'.

1808 – Agitation and demonstrations for higher wages by weavers only ended by calling out and arming the Militia

1811 – Severe distress among the poor; subscriptions set up.

1816 – More distress due to the poor harvest. 1818 – Handloom weavers demonstrate for improved pay.

1821 – Unsuccessful strike of operative spinners against 10% cut.

1823 – Unsuccessful assassination attempt on Samuel Horrocks.

1826 – New outbreak of machinery destruction in Lancashire but the Militia prevent any occurrence in Preston.

1829 – Widespread distress; soup kitchens introduced.

1831 – Rioting in Preston at the introduction of new machinery at Horrocks's 'Big factory'. 1836 – Six hundred spinners strike from November through to following February; 8,000 weavers laid off. 1840 – Decade of economic decline, the 'hungry 'forties'.

1842 – Chartist agitation and general strike; five cotton workers shot in Lune Street during a riot, by soldiers of the 72nd Highlanders on orders of the Mayor, Samuel Horrocks.

1846 – Trade depressed; two 10% wage cuts imposed.

1853 – The great 'Preston Lock-out' from October to May of the next year; 26,000 out of work. Subscriptions from around the country assist distress but resistance collapses after arrest of the leaders.

1861 – Start of American Civil War heralds the 'Cotton Famine' which lasts for five years; great distress throughout the industry, but particularly in Preston.

1862 – Earl of Derby instrumental in setting up and maintaining relief organisation.

1863 – Riot by unemployed in protest at changes in relief system.

1866 – Cotton Famine ends.

1869 – General strike commencing April; weavers out until May, spinners until September.

1878 – Second great lock-out across all Lancashire ends in failure for workers.

McCaffery

On October 10th 1860, in Liverpool, Patrick McCaffery enlisted in the 32nd Regiment of Foot (Duke of Cornwall's Light Infantry). He was posted immediately to Fulwood Barracks.

He was eighteen at the time. Brought up by his mother in Kildare, Ireland, in reduced circumstances after his civil servant father ran off to America soon after his birth, he was duly sent by her at twelve years of age to a friend in Manchester to learn a trade in a Stalybridge cotton mill.

The young teenager did not settle down and drifted in and out of employment and minor trouble in Manchester and Liverpool for the next six years. However, it would not be fair to dismiss him as a shiftless loafer; some later reports describe him as a 'bookworm' and 'of a studious turn of mind'.

Not surprisingly, it seems he was no more able to adapt to life in the army than to life in the mills. No doubt Queen's Regulations, spit and polish sat ill upon him once the novelty wore off and the Recruiting Sergeant's promises wore thin.

Worse still, the Depot Adjutant, Captain John Hanham, was, by all contemporary accounts, a peppery martinet, a rigid disciplinarian even by the standards of those stern days. McCaffery seems to have offended Hanham almost at a personal level to such an extent that over the next ten months he mounted a campaign of persecution against the young soldier, inflicting a series of humiliating punishments for minor offences, with the tacit approval of the Commanding Officer, Colonel Hugh Crofton.

The fatal drama began with a trivial incident on September 13th. McCaffery, who was on guard duty, failed to prevent some children from playing in a prohibited area near the Officers' Mess, and further compromised himself by failing to obtain the names of their soldier fathers for the enraged Hanham. The following day he found himself on another charge and the Colonel, at Hanham's insistence, confined him to barracks and docked his pay yet again.

An hour later, dressed for parade and carrying his long rifle, McCaffery saw from his open barracks window the two officers at a distance of seventy yards. He knelt, aimed and fired. The bullet tore through the Colonel's chest, through Hanham's arm and lodged in his spine. Both fell. Meanwhile McCaffery put down his weapon and awaited arrest. His only words were to declare that he had not intended to hurt the Colonel.

Within two days both officers had died of their wounds and McCaffery's fate was sealed. He was tried at Liverpool Assizes, incompetently defended and inevitably executed at Kirkdale Jail in the 11th January 1862.

One can only speculate about the soldier's state of mind at the time of the shooting. He clearly intended that Hanham should die and must have been fully aware of the penalty he would pay. He made no effort to escape and showed no signs of remorse on Hanham's account. We might reasonably conclude that Hanham had persecuted him to a point where he felt so trapped that all that remained was to destroy his tormentor even though it meant his own death. We can but guess at the motivations of Hanham.

Local opinion divided predictably, the gentry being, of course, horrified at the 'foul double murder', the working people inclining to McCaffery and unsympathetic to the officer class (the 1842 shootings were still a very real memory). In addition, he became something of a cause celebre for the large population of Irish immigrants. The song which describes the event circulated quickly in Lancashire, and gained much popularity in British Army barrack rooms, as a result of which it has spread across the world.

McCaffery

Words: From the singing of Bill McAlister, Ashton, Preston, 1968.
Tune: ibid, a variant on *Lord Franklin*, popular around 1859.

When I was eighteen years of age,
Into the army I did engage,
I left my home with good intent,
To join the 32nd Regiment.

To Fulwood barracks I then did go,
To serve my time in that depot,
But out of trouble I could not be
For Captain Hanham took a dislike to me.

As I was posted on guard one day
Some soldiers' children they came out to play.
From the Officers' Quarters my captain came,
And told me for to take those children's names.

I took one name instead of three,
With neglect of duty he then charged me.
I was confined to barracks with loss of pay,
For doing my duty in the opposite way.

For fourteen nights and thirteen days
That sentence rose and turned my brain,
To shoot my Captain dead on sight,
Was all that I could resolve at night.

I saw the Captain on the barrack square,
Walking arm-in-arm with the Colonel there,
I raised my rifle and aimed to kill,
But shot my Colonel against my will.

At Liverpool Assizes my trial I stood,
I held my courage as bet I could.
The judge, he cried, 'Now, McCaffery,
Prepare your soul for eternity'.

I have no father to take my part,
No loving mother to break her heart.
I have one friend and a girl is she
Who'd lay her life down for McCaffery.

So come all you officers, take advice from me,
And treat your men with some decency,
For it's only lies and tyranny
That made a murderer of McCaffery.

The ballad appeared soon after McCaffery's execution in 1862 (see 'McCaffery', opposite) and achieved much popularity among soldiers of the British Army, as a protest song against the brutal discipline. In this way it has travelled the world and is known and sung to this day, from New Hall Lane to New Orleans.

'A Guild Song for 1882'

Words: HBC.
Tune: Identified on the broadsheet as *Oh, Fred, tell them to stop!*,
George Meen (USA), 1879, a popular music hall hit of the day.

In the good town of Preston we're all up in arms
For this is the Guild Week you know
'Tis a holiday I'm sure never loses its charms,
Every girl gets two strings to her bow
No work can be done, it's all frolics and fun
And everyone's happy and gay.
Good luck to each Lancashire daughter and son
For we don't kill a pig every day.

   Chorus:
   Then cheer, everyone, Victoria's son,
   I think you will say that he's the best one
   If the truth we must speak, it is the Guild Week
   So we mean to be jolly in Preston.

On Monday you know, the rejoicings begin
And the banners and flags gaily fly
All the old snobs will get drunk upon gin
And the tailors will feel very dry.
Mechanics and tradesmen will march through the town
And the proud folk and Beadle as well
And every old maid will put on a new gown
And keep winking at every swell.

On Tuesday the Duke and the Duchess are here
And thousands will meet in the square
And wicked young lasses, I very much fear,
Will rumple their muslin while there
The soldiers so gay, they will trot away
Tom, Dick and Harry and Sam,
While the bobbies so bold, I have been told
In the sandhills they're looking for jam.

On Thursday the pawnshops will do a good trade
Shirts, shifts and coats will be popping
And all the Scotch duffers, I'm very much afraid,
For their money this week will be stopping.
The factory girls will trim up their curls
And down London Road to the grand
The minders and winders and other sly churls
Will ask what you're going to stand.

The Fireworks at night will be a good sight
When they're flying about in the air.
Lawyers and sawyers will get blooming tight
They can drink the sea dry I declare
Old Cetewayo would have been here
He's crying his eyes out today
He's been told Preston girls are such pretty dears
He's afraid they might lead him astray.

So we hope you may by pleasure be filled
And keep up the old holiday
You won't forget this Preston Guild
Though many years may pass away.
Be happy and free with the sights that you see
And don't get too much in your head
And when you have seen the young son of the queen
Go home with the old gal to bed.

The reference to 'Victoria's son' shows that the song was circulated in advance of Guild Week. At this point the Guild Industry had invested huge quantities of money on the basis of its planned opening by Prince Leopold, Duke of Albany (1853–1884), eighth child of Queen Victoria. Thousands of Guild medals bearing his portrait had been struck and sold. An enigmatic communication from Windsor Castle reached the Guild committee on the Friday night (the opening ceremony was scheduled for Sunday):

'Were it not for a slight indisposition,' it burbled obliquely, 'I would have enjoyed attending the Preston Guild.'

One can visualise the Cotton Lords scratching their heads over this one until the penny finally dropped.

'Does he mean he's not coming, then?'

'Aye.'

'Reet. He'll never work in Preston again!'

And nor he ever did. They booked the Earl of Lathom at very short notice, and a Birmingham foundry nearly caught fire, working frantically all weekend to produce a supply of updated commemorative medals carrying his effigy.

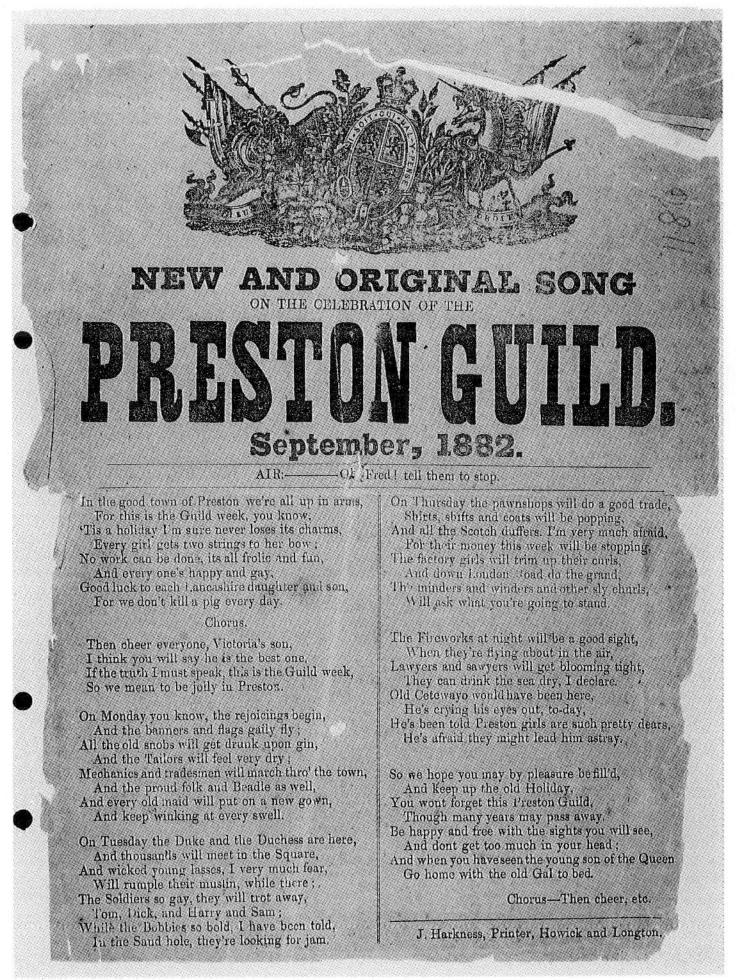

The original of Harkness's *Guild Song for 1882*.

PRESTON GUILD OF 1842

P. & H. Whittle, Printers, 25, Fishergate, Preston.

1 Now *Preston Guild* is drawing near,
  People of all sorts will be there ;
  Lords, Knights, and 'Squires of high renown,
  In Chaise and Coaches come to Town.

2 Merchants who trade beyond the seas,
  Will there attend,—their wills to please ;
  And Tradesmen, to defend their will :
  Increase the throng at *Preston Guild !*

3 The butcher's sell their meat now dear,
  They fall and rise, to spend it there,
  Their wives in Muslin will be drest,
  And Gig it away with the very best.

4 Badgers, by pinching the poor,
  And Farmer's who've got gold in store,
  And as fine as the rest, resolved they will
  Travel by Railway to *Preston Guild !*

5 The streets they'll crowded be all day.
  And every night a Ball or Play ;
  Concerts and Assemblies, then there'll be,
  Each evening to keep up the Glee.

6 With love indulging Masquerade,
  Bachelors then, are rakish blades,
  Wives, Widows, Maids. by dress and skill,
  Increase the throng at *Preston Guild !*

7 And, amongst the rest who walk you'll find,
  Adam and Eve, with the Tailors' join'd,
  With other sights more curious still,
  Increase the Show at *Preston Guild !*

8 All you that come this *Guild* to see,
  With money well provided be :
  For wanting this, your case is bad,
  You'll want both Victuals and a bed !

9 A bed of Straw or Chaff, is very high,
  And in the streets all night some lie ;
  For Barn or Stable, charge they will,
  One-shilling a night, at *Preston Guild.*

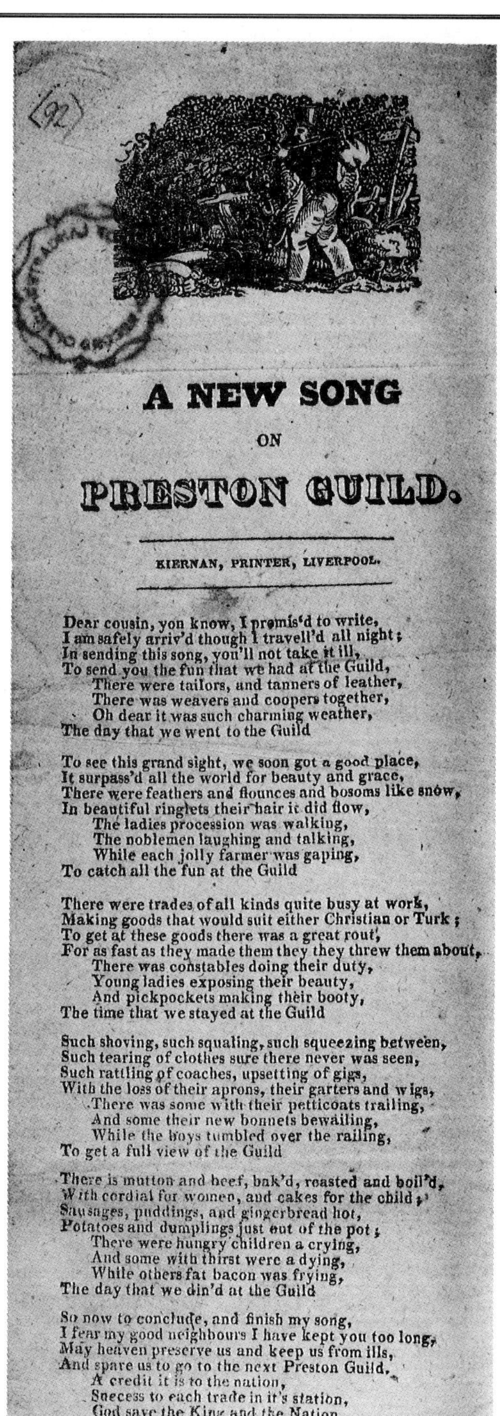

A NEW SONG

ON

PRESTON GUILD.

KIERNAN, PRINTER, LIVERPOOL.

Dear cousin, you know, I promis'd to write,
I am safely arriv'd though I travell'd all night ;
In sending this song, you'll not take it ill,
To send you the fun that we had at the Guild,
   There were tailors, and tanners of leather,
   There was weavers and coopers together,
   Oh dear it was such charming weather,
The day that we went to the Guild

To see this grand sight, we soon got a good place,
It surpass'd all the world for beauty and grace,
There were feathers and flounces and bosoms like snow,
In beautiful ringlets their hair it did flow,
   The ladies procession was walking,
   The noblemen laughing and talking,
   While each jolly farmer was gaping,
To catch all the fun at the Guild

There were trades of all kinds quite busy at work,
Making goods that would suit either Christian or Turk ;
To get at these goods there was a great rout,
For as fast as they made them they they threw them about,
   There was constables doing their duty,
   Young ladies exposing their beauty,
   And pickpockets making their booty,
The time that we stayed at the Guild

Such shoving, such squaling, such squeezing between,
Such tearing of clothes sure there never was seen,
Such rattling of coaches, upsetting of gigs,
With the loss of their aprons, their garters and wigs,
   There was some with their petticoats trailing,
   And some their new bonnets bewailing,
   While the boys tumbled over the railing,
To get a full view of the Guild

There is mutton and beef, bak'd, roasted and boil'd,
With cordial for women, and cakes for the child ;
Sausages, puddings, and gingerbread hot,
Potatoes and dumplings just out of the pot ;
   There were hungry children a crying,
   And some with thirst were a dying,
   While others fat bacon was frying,
The day that we din'd at the Guild

So now to conclude, and finish my song,
I fear my good neighbours I have kept you too long,
May heaven preserve us and keep us from ills,
And spare us to go to the next Preston Guild.
   A credit it is to the nation,
   Success to each trade in it's station,
   God save the King and the Nation,
And maintain the just rights of the Guild

lation was close to 100,000, and the mills could boast full order books. One focal point was the old Corn Exchange, complete with 1842 bullet holes, which was now converted into the nineteenth-century equivalent of the entertainment complex, a mere ninety years before the Manchester Stock Exchange copied the idea. A Guild song from Harkness echoes the Preston pride in the ancient twenty-year celebration.

Other modern features of a prosperous town began to be introduced – horse-drawn buses, post and telegraph offices. The Reverend Robert Harris, a wealthy man from his shrewd investments first in cotton and then railways, endowed the town with the technical college that later became Lancashire Polytechnic, an orphanage on Garstang Road and, of course, the library and museum (opened in 1893) that bears his name. Next to it stands the Miller Arcade, pioneering in 1895 the new steel construction techniques that were sub-sequently used for New York skyscrapers. Yet side by side with all this public building can be found the sobering statistic that the town had the highest mortality rate in the country, attributable to poor diet, poor housing and poor working conditions for many of its inhabitants.

Down on Ashton Marsh in 1885 the Prince of Wales cut the first sod to begin the largest single dock basin in the country. This was to fulfil the ambitions of the Ribble Navigation Company, which had long been looking to exploit Preston's position on the Ribble estuary. This enterprise was to hit many prob-lems on the way to its ceremonial opening in 1892, notably when the engineers discovered that the old course of the river, now cut off and stagnant, was the recipient of the flow from the town's main sewer pipes! The resulting cess-pool stopped work for three years; the smell in summer was indescribable. Eventually a new pipe was laid to Clifton Marsh and a pump found equal to the task. In fact the pump house can be seen opposite the old dock office,

Continued on page 79

The Ribble Navigation Companies And The Preston Dock

Imagine you are standing on Penwortham Hill in 1805, looking north towards the expanding town of Preston. To the right you can see the Pack Horse Bridge (at the end of what is now Broadgate) that marks the lowest dry crossing of the Ribble. The river now breaks into two channels with a wide grassy meadow between called Penwortham Holme, popular for local horse-racing. At the bottom of Fishergate Hill are some crude wharves and jetties which give way to low-lying pasture land known as Preston Marsh. At this point the channels unite again to flow in a north-westerly direction (in parallel with the modern Strand Road). After two or three hundred yards the river turns to the east by Watery Lane, passes a sturdier set of jetties known as Ashton Quays, and then winds through more broken marshland used for common grazing and looking much as Freckleton Marsh or Hesketh Bank do today. Depending on the vagaries of storm, flood or tide, it meanders, now in one channel, now in two, to its estuary at Lytham. There is modest trade at Ashton Quays for those small ships that will risk the shifting sandbanks; they sail mostly from Ireland, carrying potatoes and grain.

The history of Preston Docks begins with the first Ribble Navigation Company, which was a private venture of the major owners of the land on either side of the river from Preston to the sea. In obtaining by Act of Parliament in 1806 the rights to cut a channel for the purpose of shipping, they received the enthu-siastic support of the town's business community. The real motivation, self-interest, became clear over the

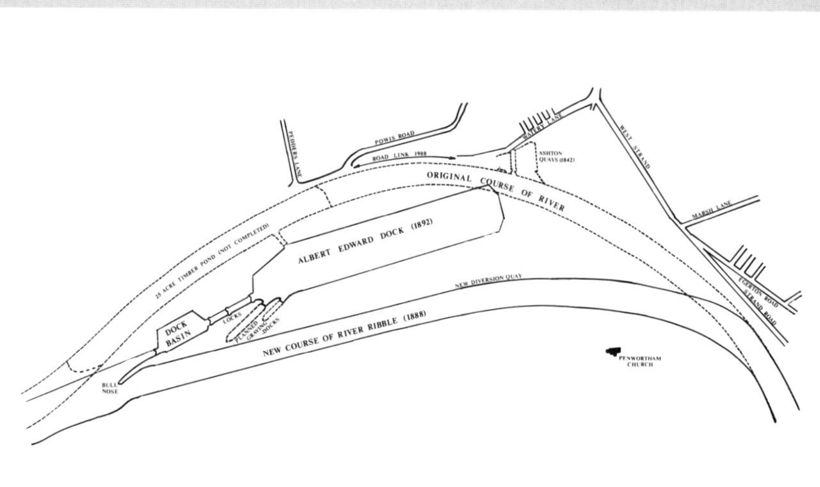

ensuing 35 years, commencing with the evidence that the worthy gentlemen wished only to channel the river to increase their pasturage by virtue of its containment, and ending with one of the them (Hesketh-Fleetwood, Preston's M.P. on several occasions) attempting to prevent any further improvement to the port in order to favour his own business venture, the town of Fleetwood. Various plans were proposed (including one for a canal to Lytham), some attempts were made to contain the river and some vessels began to use the quays on a regular basis, but by 1838 the only achievement of the company was a new stone quay at Marsh Lane and a small shipyard at the bottom of Fishergate.

In 1838 the company was revitalised by a significant injection of shareholders, notably Preston Corporation itself, to create the second Ribble Navigation Company and work began to proceed in earnest to make the river navigable. A dredger went into operation to keep the existing channel clear. At the same time a dock was opened at Lytham to shelter larger vessels waiting for the right wind and tide to proceed up-river. Lastly, a three-year plan was put into operation to straighten the course and deepen the bed of the river. The rocks that were cut from the bed were used to build up the banks and create jetties. By 1841 these operations had vastly improved and regulated the depth of the water. In 1842 a dock was cut into Ashton Quays, greatly increasing trade. In 1843 the Fishergate quays were significantly improved and several large warehouses erected, the most well-known being the bonded warehouse which until recently stood at the bottom of Marsh Lane. This brisk trading activity, which saw the landing of goods from all over the world in increasing quantities, was rewarded in 1844 by the establishment of a custom house, and in 1846 with the railway link.

The third Ribble Navigation Company came automatically into being in 1853 when the previous company fulfilled its legal term. The next decade was marked by general growth of trade combined with a consolidation of strategic real estate and the reclamation of the former marshes. The port seems to have fostered links with iron ships and paddle steamers, and there was a flourishing building and breaking business. In 1862, during the American Civil War, an ironclad blockade-runner called the *Night Hawk* was built at the Ashton Quays for the Confederate Navy. At this point we first hear the name of the engineer Edward Garlick who was to become the driving force for the building of the great dock. In 1862 he was pointing out the dangers of the main town sewage outfall which flowed untreated into the river at Ashton Quays. In 1865 he proposed the plan for diverting the course of the river to the south and using the former river bed as the basis of a large new wet dock. The next twenty years saw a downturn in trade as vessels became larger and unsuited to the existing quays; at the same time investment capital for the huge undertaking could not be raised by the existing company. In 1883 the venture was turned over in its entirety by the shareholders to the Corporation of Preston.

In 1884 the first sod was ceremoniously cut to begin the excavation of the new diversionary course for the river; the first stage of the £500,000 development scheduled to last five years. Many unforeseen difficulties were encountered, however, and by 1887 the Borough Treasurer was reporting that expenditure had already exceeded £750,000. By 1888, although the river diversion had been made operational and a quay established on it to keep the port trading, the lack of money resulted in work being suspended by a corporation pressure group calling itself 'The Party of Caution'. The contractors packed up and left (to work on the Manchester Ship Canal) and the old river course was sealed up.

Unfortunately the town's sewage continued to flow unabated from its outfalls around Ashton Quays into the now-isolated river bed to create a cesspool as big as the modern dock. With the shortage of money it was 1891 before the necessary pumping station could be put into operation, three years of misery for all Prestonians, given the prevailing westerly winds. However, once the new pump was in action the cesspool was soon cleared and the townsfolk could literally breathe easily again.

At the same time the necessary finances had been found to complete the rest of the scheme. On May 2nd 1892 the first water was carefully introduced into the forty-acre dock basin – it was vital not to let a huge surge of water bring any 'unwanted deposits' to the surface. By June the dock was completely full, and the dream of Edward Garlick fulfilled.

The glittering opening ceremony was performed on Saturday 25th June 1892 by Prince Albert, second son of Queen Victoria. There followed 89 years of trading with fluctuating success until the dock was finally closed on October 31st 1981.

displaying a fine example of the 'Lamb and Flag' motif.

And this brings us to the end of our tale, for now we are into this century and the town's continuing story can be read and heard from people who were alive to see it and take part in it. Gone is the dock, gone is the cotton industry, but in their place new industries have arisen. However, that is a tale for the future. Preston still goes on evolving, changing, adapting, like the families who make up its community, enjoying good times, living through bad. And the Guild is still celebrated every twenty years. Long may it continue.

And to end? A music hall song of the Edwardian era still popular to this day among Prestonians, who have made it their own over the years in spite of counter-claims by other Lancashire towns.

The Preston Mashers

Words: Collected by Tom Walsh from Dave Wignall of Ribbleton, 1977,
amongst many other Prestonians, too numerous to mention, but heartily
thanked.
Tune: ibid.

Now, we are the two Preston Mashers
As oft times goes out on the spree
We have no silk hats or shirts to our backs
And it's seldom we have any cash.
We always dress in the new fashions
While others they stick to the old
And though we are just twenty seven,
We're handsome, light-hearted and bold.

Chorus:
And we'll dance and we'll sing
And we don't give a jot, we're a jolly fine lot,
We're all right, when we're tight
And we're jolly fine company.

Last Saturday we were invited
To a party by two ladies fail
Their cheeks were in bloom like the roses in June
And we danced with that beautiful pair.
There was wining and dancing till midnight
There was whiskey, tobacco and rum
And after the party was over
With those ladies we had lots of fun.

And I sat over there in yon corner
With Sullivan's big wife on me knee
I knew her before she were married, I did,
And together we had many a spree.
I tickled her just out of friendship
And she tickled me back on the sly
Then I found meself under the table, I did,
With Sullivan's big boot in me eye.

Many Lancashire towns claim this song, but none so strenuously as Preston, where verses are to be found in addition to the usual two; these are mostly unsingable in delicate company. It is still a favourite for a diminishing number of Prestonians who still remember the words. Maybe it won't be lost now.

Preston in 1890
TO LANCASTER AND GLASGOW
TO LANCASTER
TO FULWOOD
TO LONGRIDGE
TO LONGRIDGE
LANCASTER CANAL
TO BLACKPOOL
TO BLACKBURN
TO THE QUAYS AND NEW DOCK WORKS
SWILL BROOK
RIVER RIBBLE
TO WIGAN
TRAMWAY (DISUSED)
RIVER DARWEN
TO SOUTHPORT
TO WIGAN AND LONDON
TO BLACKBURN
1/2 MILE
TO LIVERPOOL

Sources and Recommendations for Further Reading

Ashton, Robert, *The English Civil War* (Weidenfeld & Nicolson, 1978).

Berry, A. J., *Preston's Progress through its Gilds* (Geo. Taulmin & Sons, 1922).

Briggs, Asa, *Victorian People* (Odhams, 1954).

Victorian Cities (Odhams, 1963).

Chesney, K, *The Victorian Underworld* (Temple Smith, 1970).

Clemesha, H. W., *History of Preston in Amounderness* (Manchester University, 1912).

Dakres, J., *The Last Tide: a history of the Port of Preston* (Carnegie Press, 1986).

Delgado, A., *Victorian Entertainment* (David & Charles, Newton Abbot, 1971).

Fletcher, Anthony, *The Outbreak of the English Civil War* (Edward Arnold, 1981).

Flintoff, Thomas R., *Preston Guild Merchant* (self-published, c1952).

Hardwick, Charles, *History of the Borough of Preston and its Environs . . .* (1857).

Hewitson, Anthony, *History of Preston in the County of Lancaster* (1883).

Hobsbawm, E. J., *Labouring Men* (Weidenfeld & Nicolson, 1964).

Industry and Empire (Weidenfeld & Nicolson, 1968).

Jenkins, M., *The General Strike of 1842* (1991).

Lee, Sidney (ed.), *Dictionary of National Biography* (1891).

Lenman, Bruce, *The Jacobite Risings in Britain 16891746* (Methuen, 1980).

Lloyd, A. L., *Folk Song in England* (Lawrence & Wishart, 1967).

Pollard, W., *The Stanleys of Knowsley* (1869).

Preston and the Cotton Industry, Vols. I and II (Preston History Teachers' Association, c1982).

Sartin, Stephen, *The People and Places of Historic Preston* (Carnegie Press, 1988).

Thompson, E. P., *The Making of the English Working Class* (Penguin, 1968).

Tobias, J. J., *Crime and Industrial Society in the Nineteenth Century* (Batsford, 1967).

Tupling, G. H., *The Causes of the Civil War in Lancashire* (Lancs. & Cheshire Antiquarian Society, 1955).

Turner-Bishop, Aiden, *A Walk around the Block* (Lancashire Polytechnic, 1989).

Song Source List

AMMS *Ancient and Modern Scottish Songs*, collected by David Herd (1776; reprinted by Scottish Academic Press Ltd., Edinburgh, 1973).

BB *The Bagford Ballads*, edited by J. Woodfall Ebsworth (The Ballad Society, 1878).

BSL *Ballads and Songs of Lancashire*, John Harland (Whitaker & Co., London, 1865).

EB *The Euing Collection of English Broadside Ballads* (University of Glasgow Publications, 1971).

EBECS *Everyman's Book of English Country Songs*, Roy Palmer (J. M. Dent & Co., London, 1979).

ERVB *Elizabeth Roger Hir Virginall Booke* (c1656; reprinted by Charles J. F. Cofone, Dover Publications, New York, 1975).

FSIE *Folk Song in England*, A. L. Lloyd (Lawrence & Wishart, London, 1967).

FVB *The Fitzwilliam Virginal Book* (formerly erroneously referred to as *Queen Elizabeth's Virginal Book*) (original c1615; reprinted by Dover Publications, New York, 1963).

HBC Harkness Ballad Collection, Harris Library, Preston.

HEP Hist Eng Post Wharton

LBES *Legendary Ballads of England and Scotland*, John S. Roberts (Frederick Warne & Co., London, 1868).

LEBB *Later English Broadside Ballads*, edited by John Holloway and Joan Black (Routledge & Kegan Paul, London, 1979).

MBC Madden Ballad Collection, Cambridge University.

MDC *Merry Drollery Complete* (1691; reprinted Boston, Lincs., 1875).

PMOT *The Ballad Literature and Popular Music of the Olden Time*, William Chappell (Chappell & Co., London, 1859; reprinted Dover Publications, New York, 1965).

PBEFS *Penguin Book of English Folk Song* (Penguin Books, 1967)

PRAEP *Reliques of Ancient English Poetry*, Thomas Percy (Bernard Tauchnitz, Leipzig, 1866; reprinted by Dover Publications, New York, 1966).

SMRC *Songs and Marches of the Cavaliers and Roundheads*, Lewis Winstock (Leo Cooper, London, 1971).

SOH *Sounds of History*, Roy Palmer (Oxford University Press, Oxford, 1988).

SOTW *Songs of the Wilsons*, John Harland (Whitaker & Co., London, 1866).

TTCB *Traditional Tunes of the Child Ballads*, Bertrand Harris Bronson (Princeton University Press, 1966).

The Old Lamb and Flag

The Entertainment

As mentioned in the introduction to this book, the book itself was an offshoot of a project to provide the 1992 Preston Guild with an entertainment which would be both *for* Preston and *about* Preston, the key performance being aimed at the Charter Theatre, Preston Guild Hall, on 30th August 1992, at the start of Guild Week.

The performers, christened 'The Jolly Fine Company Company' (*cf Preston Mashers*, chorus, line 4), became the obvious candidates (as opposed to 'were selected') by having the ability, living locally, having all known each other since before the *last* Guild – but primarily by being utterly unable to say no to a new challenge.

The Jolly Fine Company Company

Gregg Butler*
Co-author, vocals, cittern, cornett, mute cornett, euphonium, records.

Malcolm Gibbons*
Vocals, guitar.

Ken Howard
Lighting, live sound production.

Chris Pollington*+
Musical director, keyboards, accordion.

Clive Pownceby
Drums, percussion.

Pat Ryan
Vocals, guitar.

Tom Walsh
Co-author, vocals, accordion, guitar, uillean pipes.

Bermard Wrigley
Narrator.

Alison Younger+
Vocals, dulcimer, recorders.

* Normally operating as Strawhead.
+ Members of First Principles and Mrs. Ackroyd's Band.

The CD and Tape

. . . were recorded at Dragontail Studios, Croston for Dragon Records of Aylesbury. Chris Pollington engineered, produced, mixed and generally 'did' the recordings over the period September 1991 to January 1992 – it would not have been possible with anyone else or in any other way, and the remainder of the JFCC hereby pay tribute.